Lynne Garton
Janice Harland

The Plant-based Plan©

Reference guide for plant-based nutrition

LANNOO
CAMPUS

D/2011/45/366 – ISBN 978 9 209 9857 3 – NUR 802

design Mo Ka & Peer De Maeyer

Publishinghouse LannooCampus
Erasme Ruelensvest 179 bus 101
B-3001 Leuven | Belgium
www.lannoocampus.com

ALPRO Foundation
Kortrijksesteenweg 1093 C
9051 Gent | Belgium
www.alprofoundation.org

Content

The Plant-based plan - Reference guide for plant-based nutrition

Introduction

For centuries many people's traditional diets have been based on plant foods and it is this particular feature which is thought to contribute to their markedly good health and long life.

Take for example the Japanese. Their health and well-being has been put down to a traditional diet based on grains, soya, fish and shellfish with less emphasis on meat and dairy products. Similarly, the traditional diets of people living in the Mediterranean region have been associated with long life expectancies and low rates of heart disease. Foods such as vegetables, fruit, legumes, nuts, whole-grains, fish and olive oil form the basis of this diet, with modest amounts of dairy foods and small amounts of meat[1]. In fact, it has been suggested that plant foods provide up to 60% of calories in this Mediterranean eating pattern with animal foods providing less than 10%[2]. Some experts would also argue that from an evolutionary perspective we are genetically programmed to eat a diet based on plant foods. Evidence for this comes from our closest living ancestors (for example wild primates) who mainly consume a plant-based diet[3,4].

As societies have become more affluent there has been a shift from these traditional diets to a more 'Western' style of eating. These Western dietary patterns are typically energy dense and made up of a higher proportion of refined foods[5]. They tend to be high in meat, dairy foods such as milk, fatty and/ or sugary foods with variable amounts of fruit and vegetables. Instead of plant foods, animal foods have become the central focus of meals and menus in this Western way of eating. Unfortunately with this shift has come an increase in lifestyle-associated diseases such as heart disease, diabetes and obesity. Experts now believe that in a land of plenty, increasing the amount of plant foods we eat would be better for our health. As a result, many international organisations and associations emphasise plant foods in their dietary recommendations to promote good health (Table 0.1).

An example of how this advice can be translated into practical suggestions is provided in the WHO countrywide integrated non-communicable disease intervention *(CINDI)* dietary guide[10]. Included within the 12 steps to healthy eating are:

- Eat a nutritious diet based on a variety of foods originating mainly from plants, rather than animals.

- Eat bread, grains, pasta, rice or potatoes several times a day.
- Eat a variety of fruits and vegetables, preferably fresh and local, several times per day (at least 400g per day).

Furthermore, international diabetes and heart associations also stress the importance of plant foods[11-13].

TABLE 0.1 – International Support for Plant-based Eating

World Health Organisation (WHO) 2004[6]	Recommendations in the Global Strategy on Diet, Physical Activity and Health report included 'Increase the consumption of fruits and vegetables, and legumes, whole grains and nuts'
World Cancer Research Fund (WCRF) 2007[7]	'Basing our diets on plant foods (like vegetables, fruits, whole-grains, and pulses such as beans), which contain fibre and other nutrients, can reduce our risk of cancer.' 'To reduce your cancer risk, eat no more than 500g (cooked weight) per week of red meats, like beef, pork and lamb, and avoid processed meats such as ham, bacon, salami, hot dogs and some sausages.'
Report of the Dietary Guidelines Advisory Committee on the Dietary Guidelines for Americans 2010[8]	'Several distinct dietary patterns are associated with health benefits, including lower blood pressure and a reduced risk of cardiovascular disease (CVD) and total mortality. A common feature of these diets is an emphasis on plant foods...' 'The totality of evidence documenting a beneficial impact of plant-based dietary patterns on CVD risk is remarkable and worthy of recommendation.'
American Dietetic Association 2009[9]	'Appropriately planned vegetarian diets, including total vegetarian or vegan diets, are healthful, nutritionally adequate, and may provide health benefits in the prevention and treatment of certain diseases'

The support for eating more plant foods, at the expense of animal foods, goes beyond the health benefits. With a growing global population, rising incomes and urbanisation, it is expected there will be an increased demand for meat[14]. Many experts agree that a continued increase in animal consumption is not sustainable for the planet. Plant foods are preferable because they require less land, water and energy resources and produce fewer greenhouse gas (GHG) emissions. In fact in 2002 the WHO reported that the rapid increase in the consumption of animal based foods, many of which are produced by intensive methods, is likely to have a number of consequences including threatening the world's ability to feed its poorest people. The report also highlighted that intensive animal rearing leads to greater environmental pressure[14]. Recently the World Wildlife Fund (WWF) launched a new report, "Livewell - a balance of healthy and sustainable food choices"[15]. This report outlined simple changes to the diet that could bring about benefits to both our health and the environment. These included:

- Eat more fruit, vegetables and cereals (especially regionally grown, in season)
- Eat less meat (meat of all kinds – red and white – are a "hotspot" in terms of environmental impact)
- Eat less highly-processed foods which tend to be more resource intensive to produce

Bringing together both the environmental and health benefits of reducing animal consumption, the UK's Chief Medical Officer quoted in his 2009 annual report '*Reducing consumption of animal products by 30% would cut GHG emissions substantially. It would reduce heart disease by 15% and would prevent 18,000 premature deaths every year[16].*'

Plant-based Diet versus Plant-based Eating?

Currently there is no exact definition of a plant-based diet, yet many people associate this way of eating with being vegetarian. However the term 'vegetarian' is very broad and encompasses a variety of eating patterns - some include variable amounts of animal foods (Table 0.2).

TABLE 0.2 – Different Types of Vegetarians

Vegans	Avoid all animal products
Lacto-ovo vegetarians	Avoid meat and fish but eat dairy foods and eggs
Lacto-vegetarians	Avoid meat, fish and eggs, but eat dairy foods
Pesco-vegetarians	Avoid meat but include fish and/or shellfish, dairy foods and eggs
Semi-vegetarians	Eat small amounts of animal products
Plant-based	At least 50% of all protein coming from plant foods [8]

While there are different ways of eating more plant foods, it is not necessary to become vegetarian to enjoy the benefits. To avoid confusion, the term 'plant-based eating' might be considered a better description. This does not necessarily exclude all animal products but places the emphasis on plant foods, as it is likely that the health benefits are associated with the quantity of plant foods eaten rather than the lack of consumption of meat[17-19]. How can this be achieved? By addressing the balance. Rather than meat being the focus of the diet, plant foods should be at the core. This advice is in line with the WCRF recommendations, suggesting that two thirds of a meal should be plant foods and one third animal products[7].

What are Plant Foods?

The good news is that plant foods are more than just fruit and vegetables. While fruit and vegetables play an important part in a plant-based eating plan, there are many other delicious foods to enjoy. The 5 major plant-based food groups that have been proposed by a group of experts include[20]:

- Whole-grains
- Legumes – including soya
- Fruit
- Vegetables
- Nuts and Seeds

This is similar to the WCRF guidelines which include vegetables, fruit, grains and cereals, pulses and roots / tubers (potatoes and yam) in the definition of plant foods[7].

Adopting a Plant-based Eating Plan

Although there is universal consensus that we should be eating more plant foods, many people find this difficult to achieve. This may be because they do not have enough information about plant-based eating or how to put it into practice[21]. Furthermore, health professionals are becoming aware of the important role they have in helping people make sustainable dietary choices. With this in mind, the Alpro Foundation is supporting health professionals to promote plant-based eating. This book is an essential reference guide providing an extensive review of the evidence supporting the nutritional, health and environmental benefits. Furthermore it helps to explain what is meant by plant-based eating and provides practical advice on how to motivate and get people started on their eating plan.

This is just the start. The Alpro Foundation is committed to providing tools to help people permanently change their diet for the better. As a result, additional on-line support is being made available which is full of practical suggestions, as well as useful tips, to make a nutritious yet delicious plant-based eating plan. It is not about transforming the diet, but by making small changes, to include more plant foods and less animal products, a big difference can be made to both our health and the planet's.

Literature Introduction

1. Trichopoulou, A. and P. Lagiou, *Healthy traditional Mediterranean diet: an expression of culture, history, and lifestyle*. Nutr Rev, 1997. **55**(11 Pt 1): p. 383-9.
2. Allbaugh LG, *Crete: A Case Study of an Underdeveloped Area*. 1953, Princeton, NJ: Princeton University Press.
3. Milton, K., *Nutritional characteristics of wild primate foods: do the diets of our closest living relatives have lessons for us?* Nutrition, 1999. **15**(6): p. 488-98.
4. Milton, K., *Micronutrient intakes of wild primates: are humans different?* Comp Biochem Physiol A Mol Integr Physiol, 2003. **136**(1): p. 47-59.
5. Prentice, A.M. and S.A. Jebb, *Fast foods, energy density and obesity: a possible mechanistic link*. Obes Rev, 2003. **4**(4): p. 187-94.
6. World Health Organisation, *Global Strategy on Diet, Physical Activity and Health*. 2004.
7. World Cancer Research Fund/American Institute for Cancer Research, *Food, Nutrition, and Physical Activity, and the Prevention of Cancer: A Global Perspective.*, in *Washington, DC: AICR*. 2007.
8. USDA (2010) *Report of the Dietary Guidelines Advisory Committee on the Dietary Guidelines for Americans, 2010.*
9. Craig, W.J. and A.R. Mangels, *Position of the American Dietetic Association: vegetarian diets*. J Am Diet Assoc, 2009. **109**(7): p. 1266-82.
10. WHO Europe. *CINDI Dietary Guide*. EURO/00/5018028 2000 January 2011]; Available from: *www.euro.who.int/document/e70041.pdf*.
11. *Lichtenstein, A.H., et al., Summary of American Heart Association Diet and Lifestyle Recommendations revision 2006. Arterioscler Thromb Vasc Biol, 2006.* ***26****(10): p. 2186-91.*
12. *Mann, J.I., et al., Evidence-based nutritional approaches to the treatment and prevention of diabetes mellitus. Nutr Metab Cardiovasc Dis, 2004.* ***14****(6): p. 373-94.*
13. *Graham, I., et al., European guidelines on cardiovascular disease prevention in clinical practice: executive summary: Fourth Joint Task Force of the European Society of Cardiology and Other Societies on Cardiovascular Disease Prevention in Clinical Practice (Constituted by representatives of nine societies and by invited experts). Eur Heart J, 2007.* ***28****(19): p. 2375-414.*
14. *Report of a Joint WHO/FAO Expert Consultation, Diet, Nutrition and the Prevention of Chronic Diseases. 2003.*
15. *WWF, Livewell: a balance of healthy and sustainable food choices. January 2011.*
16. *Dept of Health, 2009 Annual Report of the Chief Medical Officer. 2010.*
17. *Thorogood, M., et al., Risk of death from cancer and ischaemic heart disease in meat and non-meat eaters. BMJ, 1994.* ***308****(6945): p. 1667-70.*
18. *Hill, M.J., Meat and colo-rectal cancer. Proc Nutr Soc, 1999.* ***58****(2): p. 261-4.*
19. *Biesalski, H.K., Meat and cancer: meat as a component of a healthy diet. Eur J Clin Nutr, 2002.* **56 Suppl 1***: p. S2-11.*
20. *Haddad, E.H., J. Sabate, and C.G. Whitten, Vegetarian food guide pyramid: a conceptual framework. Am J Clin Nutr, 1999.* ***70****(3 Suppl): p. 615S-619S.*
21. *Lea, E.J., D. Crawford, and A. Worsley, Public views of the benefits and barriers to the consumption of a plant-based diet. Eur J Clin Nutr, 2006.* ***60****(7): p. 828-37.*

01

Chapter 01

Current Nutritional Status in Europe

Summary

- Nutrient goals have been set by both international and national organisations to help promote positive health within the population.
- Many countries in Europe fail to meet the recommendations - total and saturated fat intakes are higher, and unsaturated fats and fibre lower than recommended in most countries.
- Studies of Western European countries have found diets to be relatively high in animal, processed and sweetened/ refined foods and lacking in fruits, vegetables and other plant-based foods.
- Animal foods such as dairy foods, meat, meat products, and butter provide the majority of saturated fat in many of these Western European diets.
- A low intake of fruit, vegetables and whole-grain cereals helps to explain the poor fibre intake in many European populations.
- Translating nutritional goals into practical dietary advice for the general public has been accomplished by developing illustrated food based dietary guidelines.
- Although food-based dietary guidelines differ across Europe the main messages remain consistent and include placing the emphasis on eating plenty of plant-based foods.

Population Nutritional Goals

It's well recognised that good nutrition is one of the key factors in maintaining positive health and well-being. As such it's important to identify the optimum range of nutrient intakes for a population that is consistent with supporting good health. In Europe the most complete population nutritional guidelines are those published by the World Health Organization/ Food and Agriculture Organization of the United Nations (WHO/FAO) and Eurodiet[1,2]. The Eurodiet project started in October 1998 with the aim of contributing towards a coordinated European Union (EU) health promotion programme on nutrition, diet, and healthy lifestyles. More recently the European Food Safety Authority (EFSA) has added to these with their publication of Dietary Reference Values for fats[3], carbohydrates and dietary fibres[4].

In addition to these international guidelines, a number of national reference values exist to take into account local factors such as existing dietary intakes, cultural traditions, lifestyles and genetics. For example, the 'Dietary Reference Values for Food Energy and Nutrients for the United Kingdom' by the Department of Health, the 'Dietary reference intakes: energy, proteins, fats, and digestible carbohydrates' by the Health Council of The Netherlands and the 'Food recommendations for Belgium' by the Health Council of Belgium. As well as these national reference values, further nutrient based guidelines for groups of countries have been developed. These are the D-A-CH Reference values for the German-speaking countries and central Europe and the Nordic Nutrition Recommendations for the Nordic Countries.

Due to varying local nutritional guidelines, the international and European recommendations will be referred to in this chapter (Table 1.1) to be able to make meaningful comparisons between European countries.

Current Nutritional Status in Europe

Existing data suggests there are significant gaps between these proposed nutrient goals and actual intakes in Europe.

There are three types of data collection available for comparing food and nutrients consumption patterns across Europe; nationwide surveys of individuals, household based availability data and national food supply data. The most valuable of these comes from nationwide surveys of individuals that provide information on actual food consumption and nutrient intakes. However caution does need to be taken when interpreting and comparing this data among countries.

This is due to different methods being used to collect the information, as well as recent data not being available for all countries. Despite this, currently it's the best reflection of consumption. Using this information, a recent report on the health and nutrition status of Europe collated data by grouping different regions of the European Union and analysed the data accordingly. These groups were as follows:

- North: Denmark, Estonia, Finland, Latvia, Lithuania, Norway, Sweden
- South: Cyprus, Greece, Italy, Portugal, Spain
- Central and East: Austria, Czech Republic, Germany, Hungary, Poland, Romania, Slovenia
- West: Belgium, France, Ireland, The Netherlands, Luxembourg, United Kingdom

TABLE 1.1 – Selected Population Nutrient Based Guidelines for Europe

Nutrient	WHO[1,5,6]	Eurodiet[2]	EFSA[3,4]
Dietary Fat (%e)	15-30	< 30	20-35
Saturated Fat (%e)	< 10	< 10	Not set, but advised to be as low as possible within a nutritionally adequate diet
PUFA's (%e)	6-11	4-8%e n-6 PUFAs + 2g linolenic + 200mg LC omega-3 fats	4%e (AI) linoleic acid + 0.5%e (AI) linolenic acid + 250mg LC omega-3 fats
Cholesterol (mg/ day)	< 300		
Trans Fat (%e)	< 1	< 2	Not set, but advised to be as low as possible within a nutritionally adequate diet
Total Carbohydrates (%e)	50-75	> 50	45-60
Free Sugars (%e)	< 10		
Protein (%e)	10-15		
Fibre (g/ day)	> 25	> 25	25
Fruit and Vegetables (g/ day)	≥ 400	> 400	

%e – Percentage energy; PUFAs – Polyunsaturated fatty acids; AI – Adequate Intake (needed by the body for good health, but sufficient scientific data is not available to derive an Average Requirement, a Lower Threshold Intake or a Population Reference); LC – Long Chain, ≥20 carbon atoms

The findings suggested that for most of these European countries the percentage of energy coming from fat was above the recommended range set by WHO (28.4 to 45.0%e in males and between 29.9 to 47.2%e in females)[1]. Furthermore the fatty acid pattern did not meet the recommendations, with saturated fat intakes being higher and PUFA lower than recommended in most countries[6]. Protein intakes were within or slightly above the recommended range, whereas dietary fibre intake in most countries was lower (Table 1.2).

TABLE 1.2 – Selected Nutrient Intakes (min. – max.) in Adults Across Four European Regions Compared to International Recommendations.

Nutrient	WHO	North		South	
		Male	Female	Male	Female
Dietary Fat (%e)	15 – 30	31 – 44.9	31 – 41.9	28.4 – 45	29.9 – 47.2
Saturated Fat (%e)	< 10	12.0 – 14.6	12.0 – 14.4	8.8 – 12.7	9.4 – 13.2
PUFA's (%e)	6 – 11	4.7 – 8.9	4.7 – 8.7	4.8 – 6.4	4.5 – 6.9
Cholesterol (mg/ day)	< 300	256 – 477.9	176 – 318.8	282.9 – 378.4	227.6 – 310.8
Protein (%e)	10 – 15	13.7 – 16.8	13.7 – 17.2	14.1 – 18.5	14.4 – 19.3
Fibre (g/ day)	> 25	18.0 – 25.0	15.6 – 21.0	19.3 – 23.5	16.9 – 23.7

Nutrient	WHO	Central and East		West	
		Male	Female	Male	Female
Dietary Fat (%e)	15 – 30	31.3 – 38.9	31.2 – 39.7	34.8 – 36.5	35.1 – 36.9
Saturated Fat (%e)	< 10	11.7 – 26.3	11.7 – 24.8	13.7 – 14.6	13.7 – 14.7
PUFA's (%e)	6 – 11	5.7 – 8.8	5.6 – 9.2	6.7 – 7.0	6.7
Cholesterol (mg/ day)	< 300	352.5 – 800.0	277.0 – 680.0	250.0 – 279.0	201.0 – 215.2
Protein (%e)	10 – 15	13.5 – 17.8	13.1 – 17.1	14.7 – 16.3	15.6 – 17.0
Fibre (g/ day)	> 25	18.7 – 29.7	19.7 – 24.7	12.8 – 24.4	10.4 – 20.1

Data for individual European countries, based on individual food consumption, was also provided in the report. A similar pattern emerged for these nutrient intakes in the adult population in the UK, Netherlands, Belgium and Germany, although PUFA intake did meet the minimum recommendations. These have been compared to the recommended targets, as a percentage, in Figures 1.1 and 1.2.

FIGURE 1.1 – Selected Nutrient Intakes for Adult Men as a Percentage of the Recommended Amounts

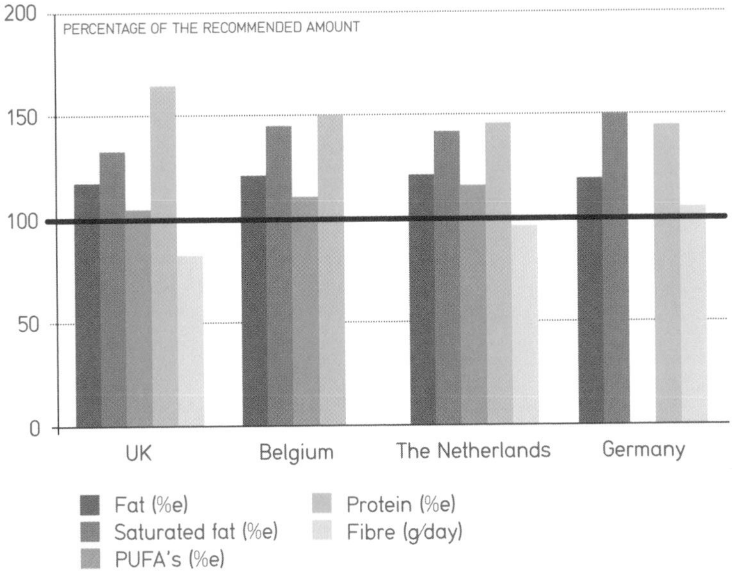

Recommended targets based on WHO ranges: Dietary fat 30%e, saturated fat 10%e, PUFA's 6%e (minimum), Protein 10%e, Fibre 25g/d (except for the UK where 18g was used to allow for the difference in fibre analysis). Data not available: fibre intake in Belgium and PUFA in Germany
Source: European Nutrition and Health Report 2009[7], UK National Diet and Nutrition Survey (NDNS) 2003[8], Die Ernährung in Deutschland, 1998

As previously highlighted, it is difficult to make direct comparisons between these countries due to differences in the dietary survey methodologies. However, the European Prospective Investigation into Cancer and Nutrition (EPIC) study uses a consistent methodology across the participating countries to collect dietary data. As a result, more meaningful comparisons can be made. Information collected in this way shows similar results, in that The Netherlands, UK and Germany are consuming too much fat and saturated fat and not enough fibre or PUFAs compared to the recommendations (Figures 1.3 and 1.4)[9-11]. Out of these selected countries, the only group that appears to meet the recommended ranges is the UK health-conscious group. This group includes lacto-ovo vegetarians, pure vegans, fish (but not meat) eaters and meat eaters. Their relatively low intake of animal products and fairly high intake of legumes[12] may account for these nutritional differences.

FIGURE 1.2 – Selected Nutrient Intakes for Adult Women as a Percentage of the Recommended Amounts

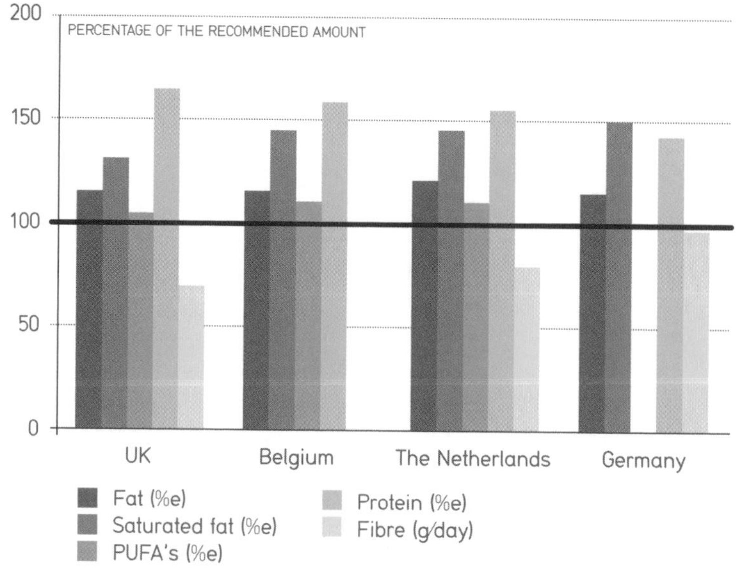

Recommended targets based on WHO ranges: Dietary fat 30%e, saturated fat 10%e, PUFA's 6%e (minimum), Protein 10%e, Fibre 25g/d (except for the UK where 18g was used to allow for the difference in fibre analysis) – Data not available: fibre intake in Belgium and PUFA in Germany

Source: European Nutrition and Health Report 2009[7], UK National Diet and Nutrition Survey 2003[8], Die Ernährung in Deutschland, 1998

FIGURE 1.3 – Mean Selected Nutrient Intakes in Men in the EPIC study

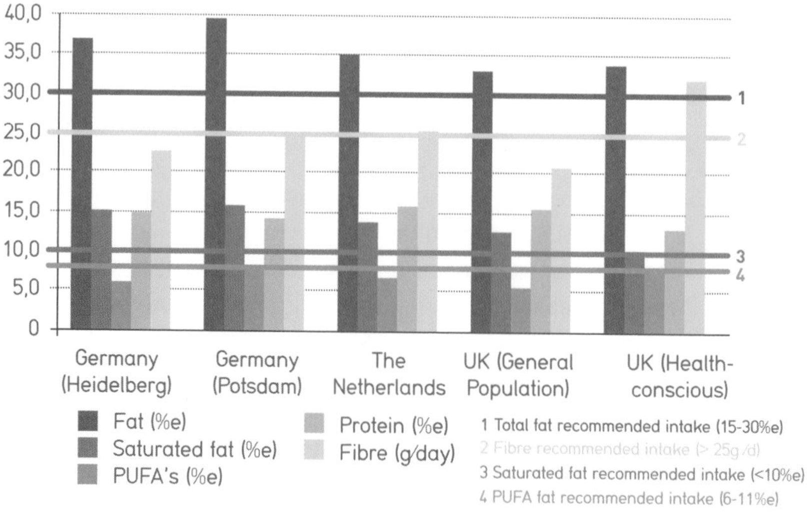

FIGURE 1.4 – Mean Selected Nutrient Intakes in Women in the EPIC study

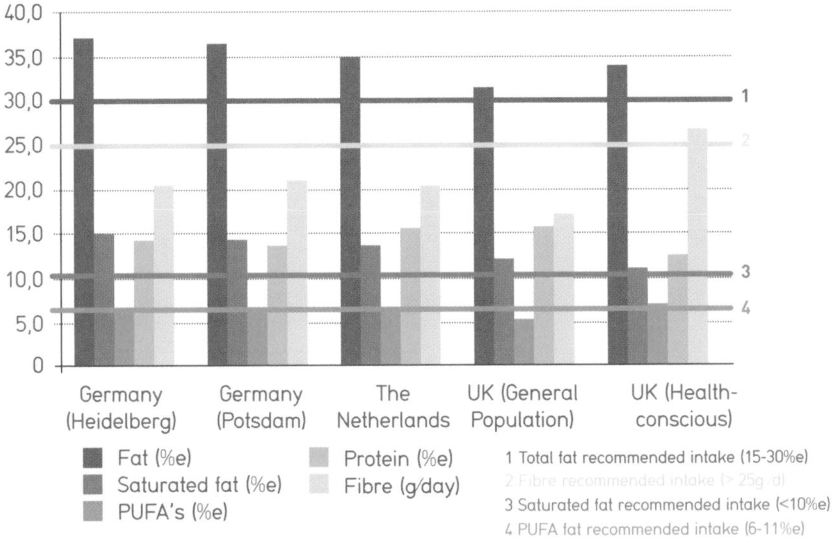

Main Challenges to Nutrient Intake

To help improve public health, the key priorities for many Western European populations is to tackle the over consumption of fat, particularly saturated fat, and to improve the fat quality and lack of fibre in the diet. To be able to do this it's helpful to identify and quantify the main food sources of these nutrients. This in turn can help formulate food-based dietary guidelines to enable nutrient goals to be met.

Saturated Fat

Data from the EPIC study suggests that a large percentage of saturated fats come from animal products, including dairy foods, meat, meat products, and butter in a number of European countries (Figures 1.5 and 1.6)[11]. Approximately two-thirds of the total saturated fat in the diet came from these foods in Germany, while in The Netherlands they provided over half and in the UK general population they contributed just under half of the total saturated fat intake. In contrast, in the UK health-conscious group these foods only provided around a third of the total saturated fat in the diet.

FIGURE 1.5 – Average Contribution of Major Food Groups to Saturated Fat Intake in Men from Selected Countries Participating in the EPIC Study

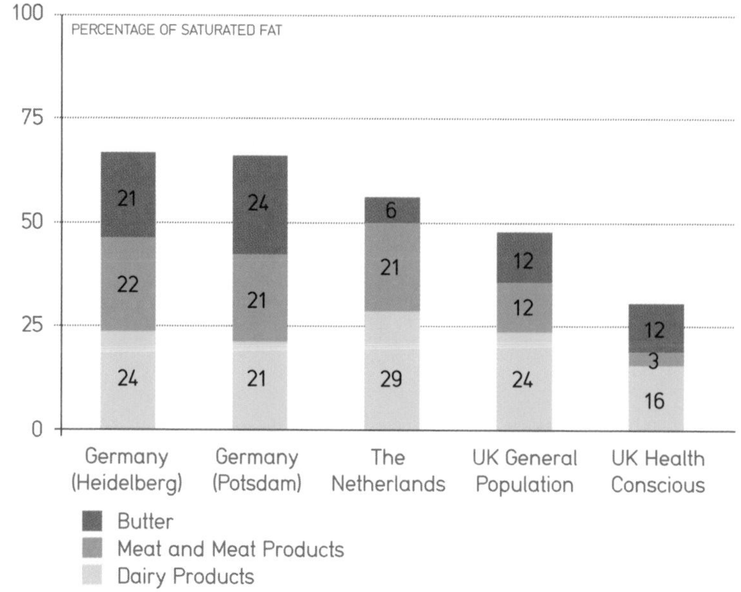

FIGURE 1.6 – Average Contribution of Major Food Groups to Saturated Fat Intake in Women from Selected Countries Participating in the EPIC Study

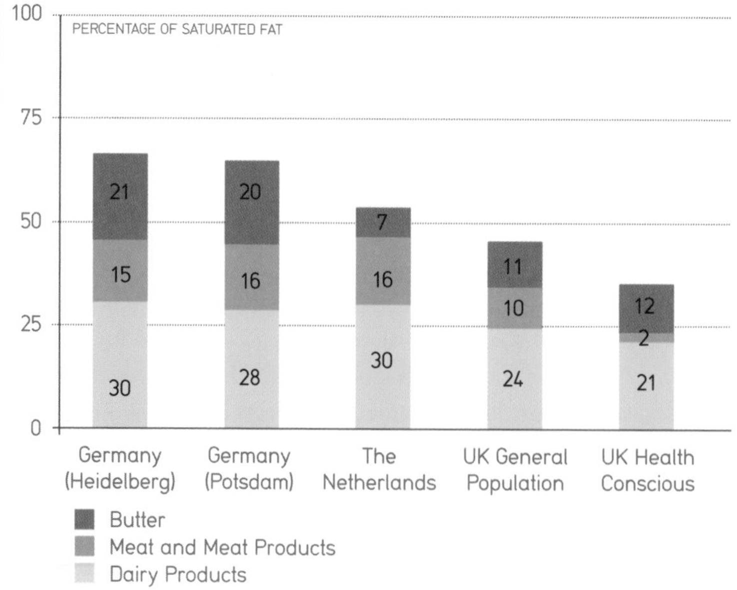

This data is supported by national dietary surveys. For example in the UK's NDNS[8] meat products, dairy foods and butter provided 52% of the total saturated fat intake (22%, 24% and 6% respectively). In the latest NDNS rolling programme, this remained at 52%, however the food contributions changed – meat products provided 26%, dairy products 22% and butter 4%[13]. However caution does need to be taken when interpreting this more recent data as the results of this survey may not be entirely representative of the UK population due to the small sample size of the current programme. Furthermore different methodologies have been used in these two dietary surveys.

Considering these foods contribute to the majority of saturated fats in the diet, dietary recommendations emphasise only modest amounts should be included as part of a healthy, balanced diet and that lower fat options such as low fat dairy foods and dairy alternatives, low in saturated fat (e.g. soya), should be chosen. Instead more plant-based foods are encouraged to make up the bulk of the diet. Shifting towards plant-based eating would subsequently reduce fat and saturated fat intakes, increase polyunsaturated fats, while at the same time help to achieve fibre targets.

Although international and national recommendations suggest a reduction in animal product consumption, no exact figures have been suggested as a target. However a number of organisations have given guidance on meat intake. For example, in 2007 the World Cancer Research Fund recommended that red meat consumption be limited to 500g (cooked weight) per person per week, as well as avoiding processed meats, in order to significantly reduce the risk of cancer[14]. As a population goal this should be reduced to 300g/week. In its review on iron and health, the UK's Scientific Advisory Committee on Nutrition (SACN) advised, as a precaution, that intakes of red and processed meat not to increase above 70g/day[15]. Red meat usually refers to beef, goat, lamb, pork and processed meat refers to meat (usually red) that has been preserved by smoking, curing, salting, or addition of preservatives[14].

How do these recommendations compare to current meat intakes in Europe? This is hard to measure accurately as comparing intakes across countries is difficult due to different definitions of meat. However a recent review on red meat in the diet attempted to do this and used the EPIC results for European intakes due to its consistent methodology (Figure 1.7)[16]. Unfortunately this is relatively old data and more up-to-date figures from EPIC are currently not available.

FIGURE 1.7 – Average Daily Intake of Red Meat and Processed Meat in Selected Countries

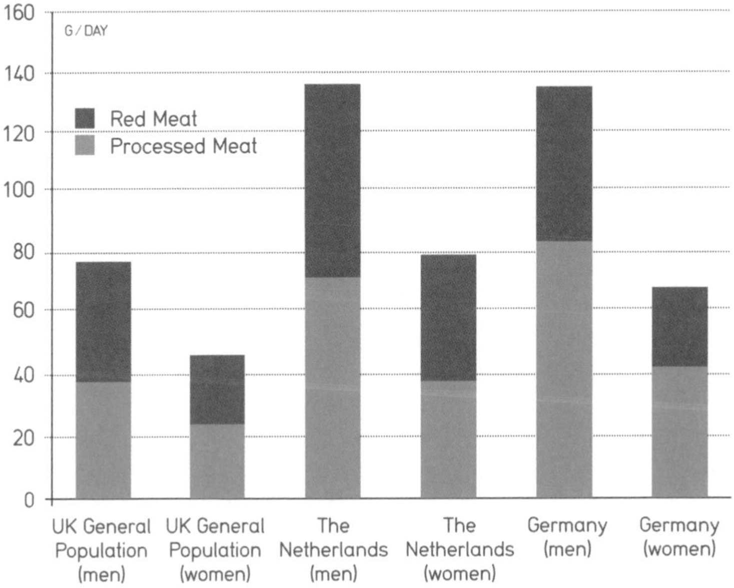

Another method for determining meat intakes is to look at the data collected in national dietary surveys which include individuals' food consumption. However, as mentioned previously this is problematic due to different methodologies and definitions of foods. Nevertheless, in an attempt to harmonise this, the European Food Safety Authority (EFSA) has compiled the available data from these surveys in a way to make it as comparable as possible across Europe (EFSA Concise Database)[17]. Using this database, population intakes of meat, meat products and offal for selected countries are detailed in Figure 1.8.

The most recent UK data on red meat consumption has been calculated by SACN in their 2010 report on iron and health. After adjusting NDNS figures from 2000/01 and 2008/09 surveys (in an attempt to make them comparable) they found total red and processed meat had increased by more than 10g/person/day over this time period (70g/ day to 83.1g/ day). However they do state that due to differences in survey methodologies these findings should be interpreted very cautiously[15].

FIGURE 1.8 – Average Adult Daily Consumption of Meat, Meat Products and Offal (g/ day) in Selected Countries

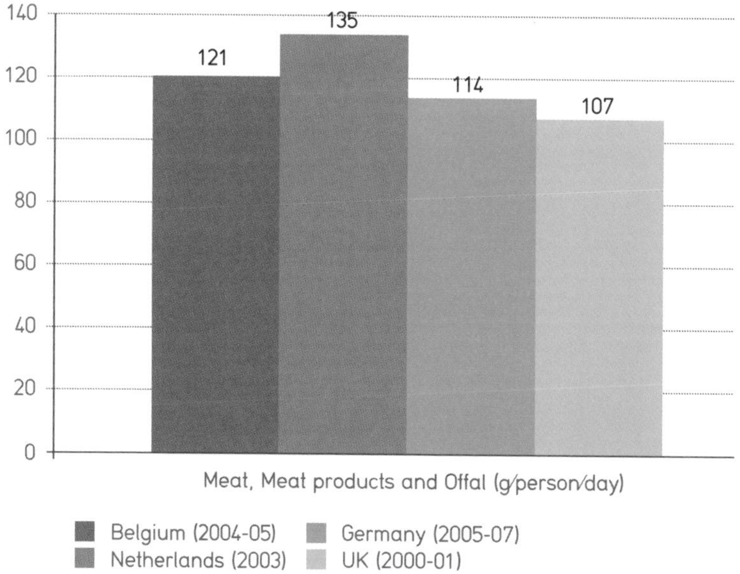

Source: EFSA, Concise European Food Consumption Database[17]

Unsaturated Fats

Many Western European countries fail to reach the recommendation for PUFA intake. Furthermore the importance of replacing saturated fat with unsaturated fat has been recognised as an important aspect in heart health (see Chapter 04). A recent analysis that compared the ratio of saturated fat to unsaturated fat among different countries found an unfavourable result (> 0.5) in most European countries[18]. This situation could be improved by including more foods such as nuts, seeds, vegetable oils and legumes into the diet at the expense of animal fats.

Fibre

Fibre is found exclusively in plant foods and good sources include fruit, vegetables, whole-grains and pulses. Consequently the WHO has concluded that whole-grain cereals, fruits and vegetables should be the preferred sources of fibre in the diet[1].

Fruit and Vegetables

Although recommendations have been made for fruit and vegetable intakes (≥ 400g/ day), data from the EPIC study suggests a number of European countries fail to meet this target (Figure 1.9)[19].

Figure 1.9 – Mean Consumption of Fruit and Vegetables (Grams) per Person per Day in Selected Countries Participating in the EPIC Study

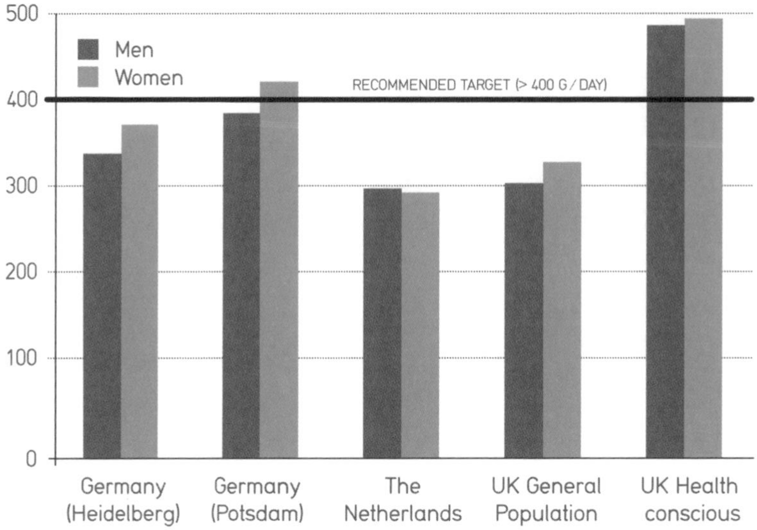

This is also confirmed in national dietary surveys. For example a study conducted in Belgium concluded that average fruit and vegetable consumption was only 256g/ day (118g/ day for fruit and 138g/ day for vegetables)[20]. Furthermore in the last full survey of the UK's NDNS, average fruit and vegetable consumption was fewer than three portions (a portion equating to 80g) of fruit and vegetables a day (2.7 and 2.9 for men and women respectively)[21]. Although the more recent NDNS (2008/2009)[13] indicated that this intake had increased to an average of 4.4 portions a day, as explained previously caution needs to be taken when interpreting these more recent results. Furthermore a different approach was used to calculate these more recent fruit and vegetable intakes, making it difficult to make like for like comparisons.

Whole-grains

Many international and national associations recommend the inclusion of more whole-grains into the diet (see Introduction) and evidence from epidemiological data suggest that the amount needed to benefit health is three or more portions of whole-grain foods a day. Generally in Western countries this goal is not being achieved. For example, in the UK adults on average consume less than one serving of whole-grains a day, 84% consume less than the recommended 3 servings a day and 29% do not consume any whole-grains at all[22].

Dietary Patterns across Europe

Examining dietary patterns also provides information on a population's food, and subsequent nutrient, intake. The EPIC study has examined these patterns across European countries and found that the diet in the Nordic countries, The Netherlands, Germany and the UK general population is relatively high in potatoes and animal, processed and sweetened/ refined foods. Vegetable oils and legumes are eaten in smaller amounts. As highlighted previously, the UK health-conscious group have a relatively low intake of animal products and higher intakes of legumes compared to the UK general population[12].
Household-based availability data (using household budget surveys) provides a second valuable source of food availability at household level. The data food networking (DAFNE) project aims to standardise the data collected in these surveys and has created a regularly updated food databank of comparable data from a number of European countries. In the health and nutrition status of Europe report, this data was used to calculate intakes of plant and animal foods across the four European Regions previously described[7]. Figures 1.10 and 1.11 highlight how intake of vegetables, pulses and fruits are lowest in the Western countries, while dairy, meat and meat products are among the highest in this region.

Translating the Science into Practical Dietary Advice

To be understood by the public, nutrient goals need to be translated into relevant and meaningful food based dietary guidelines. These need to include information on the contribution of different foods or food groups to an overall diet that help to maintain good health through optimal nutrition.
Recently the European Commission requested EFSA to provide guidance on developing food based dietary guidelines intended for the European population

FIGURE 1.10 – Mean Availability (g/ person/ day) of Foods of Plant Origin by European Region. The DAFNE databank

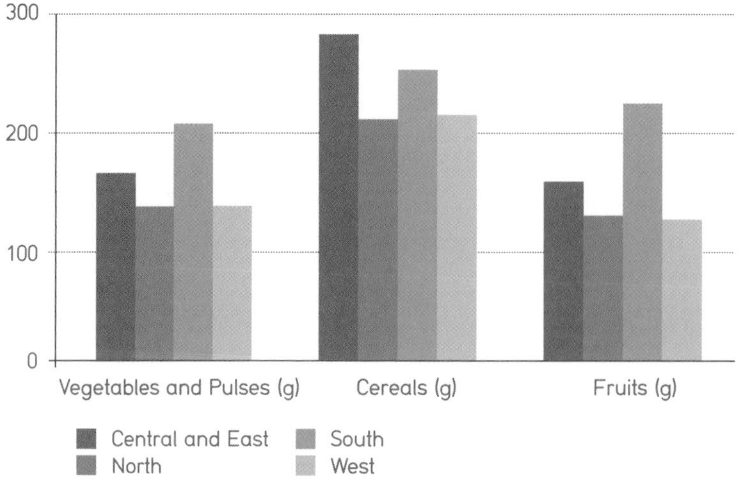

FIGURE 1.11 – Mean Availability (g/ person/ day) of Foods of Animal Origin by European Region. The DAFNE databank

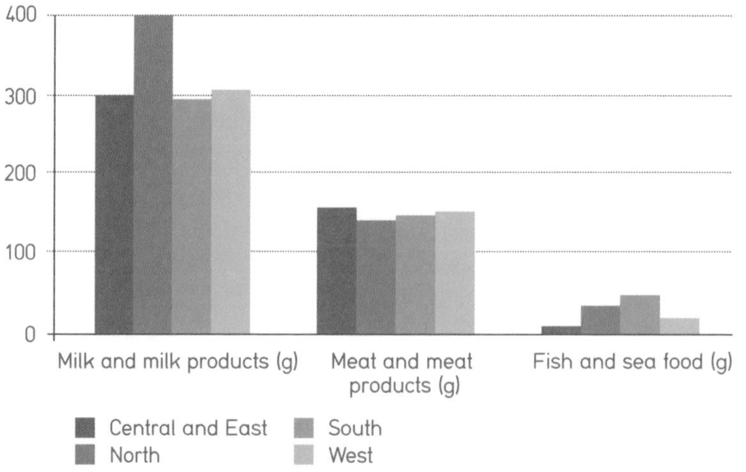

as a whole. However due to the diverse nutrient intake and public health priorities across the region, as well as differences in cultural/ dietary habits, EFSA felt it was not feasible to establish detailed and effective food-based dietary guidelines which could be used at the EU level. Instead guidelines have been provided on how an effective model can be produced[23].

Nearly all European countries have developed food based dietary guidelines. Many countries base their guidelines on the WHO Food Pyramid (Figure 1.12) from the Countrywide Integrated Non Communicable Disease Intervention (CINDI) programme[24], for example Belgium (Figure 1.13). Other countries slightly adapt this model e.g. Germany uses a three-dimensional model (Figure 1.14). Countries such as the UK use a plate model (Figure 1.15). Different size segments represent the proportions these foods should be eaten as part of a healthy balanced diet.

FIGURE 1.12 – WHO Food Pyramid

FIGURE 1.13 – Belgium's Food Pyramid

FIGURE 1.14 – Germany

FIGURE 1.15 – UK's Eatwell Plate

Common recommendations in all these models include eating plenty of fruits, vegetables and complex carbohydrates, and choosing foods which are lower in saturated fat, salt and sugar. Animal foods, including meat and dairy, represent smaller segments in these models highlighting that only modest amounts are required as part of a healthy balanced diet. In contrast, plant-based foods represent larger segments.

A couple of attempts have been made to compare these guidelines with actual intakes of foods and drinks in the diet. For example a study that evaluated the gap between usual food consumption and the guidelines in Belgium found that fruit, vegetables, dairy and calcium enriched soya was less than that recommended. Whereas meat and meat related foods, and energy-rich/ nutrient-poor foods was in excess. This was then depicted graphically based on Belgium's food model (Figure 1.16)[20].

FIGURE 1.16 – Variations in Food Consumption versus Food Recommendations in Belgium

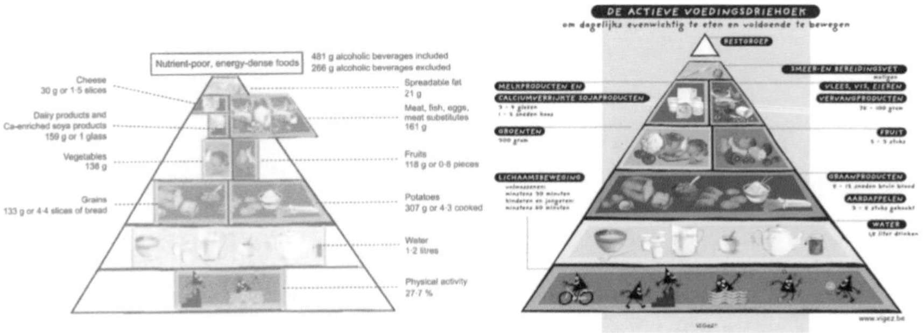

In the development of a sustainable 'livewell' diet (an eating plan that is both healthy and sustainable for the planet), the World Wildlife Fund modelled the UK's actual food intake and compared it to the segments in the national Eatwell Plate. Using consumption data from the NDNS, they concluded that the meat group as well as food and drinks high in fat and sugar were in excess of the recommendations whereas fruit, vegetables and starchy foods were not sufficient (Figure 1.17)[25].

This imbalance in food groups, and subsequent nutrient intakes, are the focus of many public health campaigns across Europe. Driving these forward will improve the overall quality of the diet, help to achieve the ideal nutrient goals, and enable populations to enjoy positive health and well-being.

FIGURE 1.17 – The UK Diet Displayed in the Eatwell Plate Food Groups

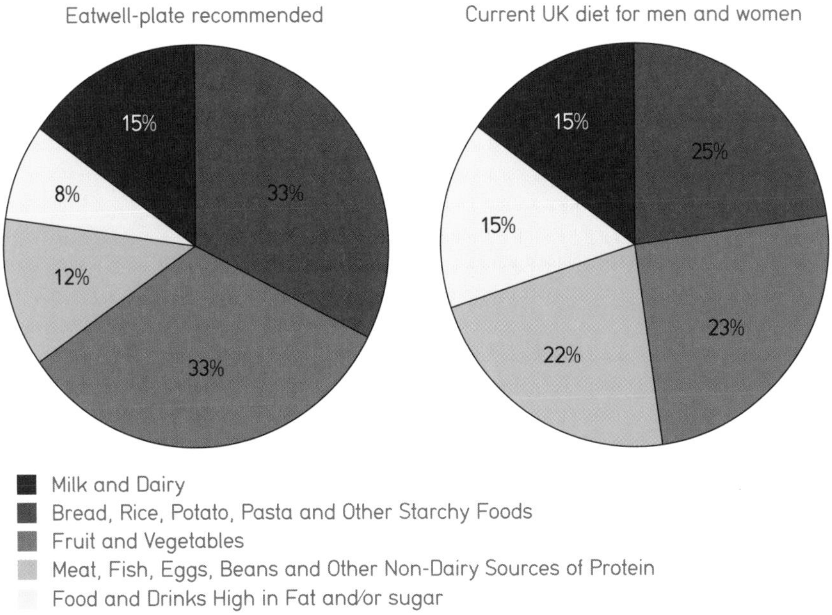

Source: WWF report, Livewell: a balance of healthy and sustainable food choices[25]

Diets in many Western European countries are higher in total fat and saturated fat and lower in fibre and unsaturated fat than is recommended for good health.

Eating smaller amounts of animal foods, which are the main sources of saturated fats in many of these diets, and replacing these with legumes, nuts, oils and seeds can improve the quality of the diet and help achieve current dietary recommendations.

Dietary quality can also be enhanced by consuming more fruits, vegetables and other fibre-rich foods such as whole-grain cereals.

Ensuring there are more plant foods in the diet is a simple and delicious way of improving the health of the nation.

Literature chapter 01

1. World Health Organisation (WHO)/FAO Diet, Nutrition and the Prevention of Chronic Diseases. Report of a Joint WHO/FAO Expert Consultation. 2003, World Health Organ Tech Rep Ser 916:i-vii, 1-149.
2. Eurodiet core report, Nutrition & Diet for Healthy Lifestyles in Europe. 2000, Science and Policy Implications, University of Crete School of Medicine (coord.), Greece.
3. EFSA Panel on Dietetic Products Nutrition and Allergies (NDA), Scientific Opinion on Dietary Reference Values for fats, including saturated fatty acids, polyunsaturated fatty acids, monounsaturated fatty acids, trans fatty acids, and cholesterol EFSA Journal,, 2010. 8(3): p. 1461. [107 pp.].
4. EFSA Panel on Dietetic Products Nutrition and Allergies (NDA), Scientific Opinion on Dietary Reference Values for carbohydrates and dietary fibre. EFSA Journal,, 2010. 8(3):1462. [77 pp.].
5. World Health Organization (WHO), Joint FAO/WHO Scientific update on carbohydrates in human nutrition. Eur J Clin Nutr, 2007. 61(Suppl 1).
6. World Health Organization (WHO), Joint FAO/WHO Expert Consultation on fats and fatty acids in human nutrition. Ann Nutr Metab, 2009. 548(Suppl 3).
7. Elmadfa, I., et al., European Nutrition and Health Report 2009. Forum Nutr, 2009. 62: p. 1-405.
8. Henderson L, The National Diet and Nutrition Survey: Adults Aged 19-64Y. Volume 2 Energy, Protein Carbohydrate, Fat and Alcohol Intake. . 2003, The Stationary Office:London.
9. Ocke, M.C., et al., Energy intake and sources of energy intake in the European Prospective Investigation into Cancer and Nutrition. Eur J Clin Nutr, 2009. 63 Suppl 4: p. S3-15.
10. Cust, A.E., et al., Total dietary carbohydrate, sugar, starch and fibre intakes in the European Prospective Investigation into Cancer and Nutrition. Eur J Clin Nutr, 2009. 63 Suppl 4: p. S37-60.
11. Linseisen, J., et al., Dietary fat intake in the European Prospective Investigation into Cancer and Nutrition: results from the 24-h dietary recalls. Eur J Clin Nutr, 2009. 63 Suppl 4: p. S61-80.
12. Slimani, N., et al., Diversity of dietary patterns observed in the European Prospective Investigation into Cancer and Nutrition (EPIC) project. Public Health Nutr, 2002. 5(6B): p. 1311-28.
13. Bates B, National Diet and Nutrition Survey. Headline results from Year 1 of the Rolling Programme (2008/2009). 2010, Food Standards Agency/ Department of Health: London.

14. World Cancer Research Fund/American Institute for Cancer Research, Food, Nutrition, and Physical Activity, and the Prevention of Cancer: A Global Perspective., in Washington, DC: AICR. 2007.

15. Scientific Advisory Committee on Nutrition. SACN report on iron and health. 2010 February 2011]; Available from: http://www.sacn.gov.uk/pdfs/sacn_iron_and_health_report_web.pdf.

16. Wyness L, e.a., Red meat in the diet: an update. Nutrition Bulletin, 2011. 36: p. 34-77.

17. European Food Safety Authority (EFSA). Concise European Food Consumption Database. Accessed February 2011]; Available from: http://www.efsa.europa.eu/en/datex/datexfooddb.htm.

18. Elmadfa, I. and M. Kornsteiner, Dietary fat intake--a global perspective. Ann Nutr Metab, 2009. 54 Suppl 1: p. 8-14.

19. Agudo, A., et al., Consumption of vegetables, fruit and other plant foods in the European Prospective Investigation into Cancer and Nutrition (EPIC) cohorts from 10 European countries. Public Health Nutr, 2002. 5(6B): p. 1179-96.

20. Vandevijvere, S., et al., The gap between food-based dietary guidelines and usual food consumption in Belgium, 2004. Public Health Nutr, 2009. 12(3): p. 423-31.

21. Henderson L, The National Diet & Nutrition Survey: Adults Aged 19 to 64Y. Vol 1 Types and quantities of foods consumed. 2002, The Stationary Office: London.

22. Thane, C.W., et al., Comparative whole-grain intake of British adults in 1986-7 and 2000-1. Br J Nutr, 2007. 97(5): p. 987-92.

23. EFSA, EFSA Panel on Dietetic Products, Nutrition and Allergies (NDA) ; Scientific Opinion on establishing Food-Based Dietary Guidelines. EFSA Journal,, 2010. 8(3): p. 1460.

24. WHO Europe. CINDI Dietary Guide. EURO/00/5018028 2000 January 2011]; Available from: www.euro.who.int/document/e70041.pdf.

25. WWF, Livewell: a balance of healthy and sustainable food choices. January 2011.

02

Chapter 02

Nutritional Rationale for Plant-Based Eating

Summary

- Plant-based eating is associated with a diet that is low in total fat and saturated fat, a good source of unsaturated fats, and high in fibre which is in line with international and national dietary recommendations.
- Plant foods provide a wide range of nutrients that are thought to contribute to positive health and well-being.
- Plant-based eating encompasses a spectrum of dietary practices from the complete exclusion of animal products through to small amounts of meat being eaten in the diet.
- Depending on the extent to which animal products are excluded from the diet, consideration will need to be given on replacing certain nutrients with plant sources.
- Appropriately planned plant-based eating patterns are both healthy and can meet nutritional requirements throughout the lifecycle.

Contrary to the typical 'Western' style of eating, plant-based eating patterns are associated with diets that are low in total and saturated fat, good sources of unsaturated fats (both omega-3 and omega-6 fatty acids), high in fibre, antioxidant vitamins and phytonutrients[1]. As such, these eating patterns are in line with international and national dietary recommendations (see Chapter 01). Evidence for this is supported by a number of population studies[2-9]. For example, dietary characteristics were examined in the Oxford arm of the European Prospective Investigation into Cancer and Nutrition (EPIC) study[2]. Subjects included meat-eaters (n=33,883), fish eaters (n=10,110), lacto-ovo vegetarians (n=18,840) and vegans (n=2596). The nutritional content of these diets are outlined in Figures 2.1 and 2.2. Of particular note is that the average saturated fat intake in vegans was approximately 5% of calories, less than half that of meat eaters (10-11%). Saturated fat intakes in fish eaters and vegetarians were intermediate at approximately 9% of calories. In addition, polyunsaturated fat intake was highest in the vegan group, followed by fish eaters and vegetarians. Meat-eaters had the lowest intake. Fibre was also highest in the vegan group, followed by vegetarians and fish-eaters, while meat eaters consumed the least amount of fibre.

This same nutritional pattern has also been observed in self-defined vegetarians who include small amounts of meat in their diet. A study involving 2,516 US men and women, aged between 15 and 23 years, found that current vegetarians had healthier dietary intakes than non-vegetarians with regard to fruits, vegetables and fat[3]. Data was obtained from a population based study in Minnesota (Project EAT-II: Eating Among Teens) where participants completed a mailed survey and food frequency questionnaire in 2004. Vegetarian status was self-reported and was divided into 3 categories – current, former and never vegetarians. Of those who identified themselves as current vegetarians: 94.3% reported consuming milk products, 87.3% reported consuming some eggs, 46% reported consuming fish and 25.1% reported eating chicken. In the current vegetarian group average daily intake of fruit and vegetables was approximately 5 portions/ day compared to between 3 and 4 in the former or never vegetarian group. In the younger vegetarian age group, 28.6% of energy (%e) came from total fat and 10.3%e from saturated fat, compared to 30.7% and 11% respectively in the never vegetarians. In the older age group, current vegetarians consumed 24.7%e from total fat and 8.4%e from saturated fat, compared to 30.9%e and 10.7%e respectively in the older, never vegetarian group.

FIGURE 2.1 – Men's Average Daily Intake of Selected Nutrients by Diets in the Oxford arm of the EPIC study

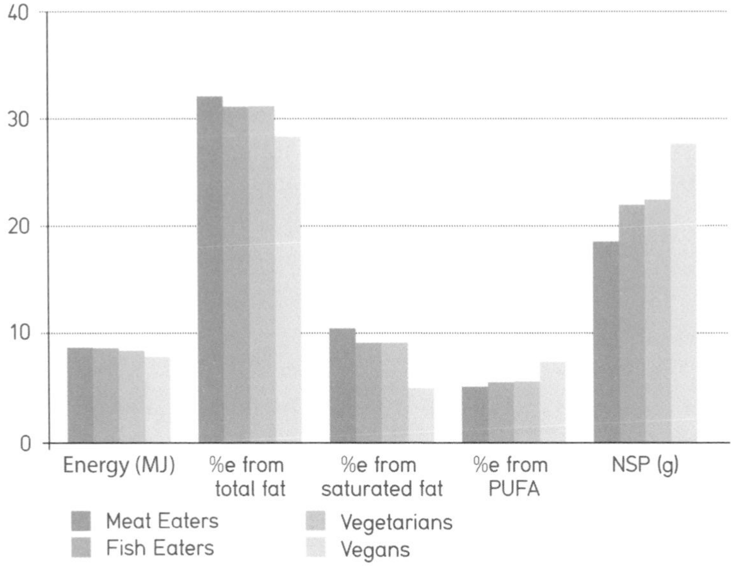

FIGURE 2.2 – Women's Average Daily Intake of Selected Nutrients by Diets in the Oxford arm of the EPIC study

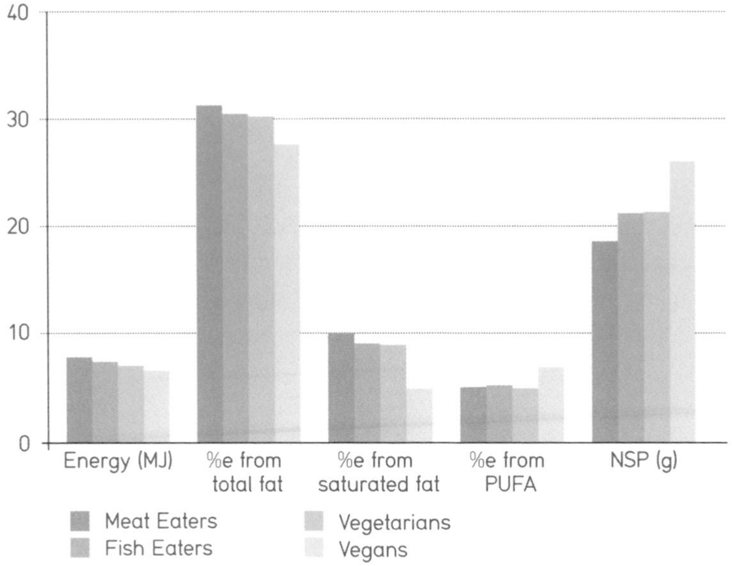

%e – Percentage Energy; PUFA- polyunsaturated fatty acids; NSP – Non-Starch Polysaccharides

Meat-eating vegetarians have also been observed in other studies[4,10-12]. For example, data from 13,313 US participants, over the age of 6 years, in the Continuing Survey of Food Intake by Individuals (CSFII) was used to compare self-defined vegetarian and non-vegetarian dietary patterns[4]. The vegetarian and non-vegetarian dietary classifications were further divided into groups who either ate 'no meat' or 'ate meat' based on results from two, 24 hour dietary recalls. Approximately two thirds of the sample population who classified themselves as vegetarians in fact ate meat. Diets of self-defined vegetarians who included meat tended to be lower in total fat, saturated fat and cholesterol, and higher in fibre than the diets of non-vegetarians who ate meat (Table 2.1).

TABLE 2.1 – Average Daily Intake of Selected Nutrients of Diets by Self-defined Vegetarian Status

Nutrient	Self-defined meat eater	Self-defined vegetarian (ate meat)
Total fat (%e)	32.9	30.2
Saturated fat (%e)	11.1	9.6
Cholesterol (mg)	267	238
PUFA (%e)	6.5	7
Fibre (g/ 2000kcals)	15.3	19.5

These vegetarians ate significantly less meat (160g/ day versus 216g/ day), red meat (80g versus 137g/ day) and poultry (42g versus 57g) but more fish (38g versus 22g/ day) than non-vegetarians. Furthermore, they reported to eat whole-wheat bread, brown rice, soya milk, meat substitutes, lentils, chickpeas, walnuts and pecans more frequently. The authors concluded that self-defined vegetarians may consume red meat, poultry or fish and their dietary and nutrient patterns are generally better than those of non-vegetarians.
Plant-based eating patterns are in line with this - based on plants, but not exclusively so.

Improving the Fat Profile of the Diet with Plant Foods

Currently many Western countries are consuming diets too high in saturated fat, with large amounts coming from animal based foods and drinks (see Chapter 01). It is thought that the lower intake of saturated fat in plant-based eating patterns may be due to plant foods displacing other foods in the diet that are

high in saturated fat. This was explored in a study led by Professor Jenkins from the University of Toronto[13]. He devised a diet that contained foods representative of foods typically eaten in the US diet, providing approximately 33% of calories from total fat and 11% from saturated fat. He then calculated the effect of substituting animal sources of protein (such as milk, yoghurts, steak and bacon) with equivalent amounts of soya protein (13-58g/ day). He determined that a 13g/ day soya substitution would result in a reduction in saturated fat from approximately 11% of calories to 8%. This would be further lowered to 5.8% of calories if 58g of soya was substituted. Dietary cholesterol would also be reduced from 316mg/ day to between 205 to 267mg/ day. Whereas polyunsaturated fats would increase from 5.7%e to between 7.5 to 8.0%e.
Figure 2.3 further highlights the reductions in saturated fat that could be achieved if certain foods were 'swapped' with plant-based (soya) alternatives.

Figure 2.3 – Saturated Fat Content (g) of Various Animal Based Products Compared to Soya Alternatives (Available on the UK Market)

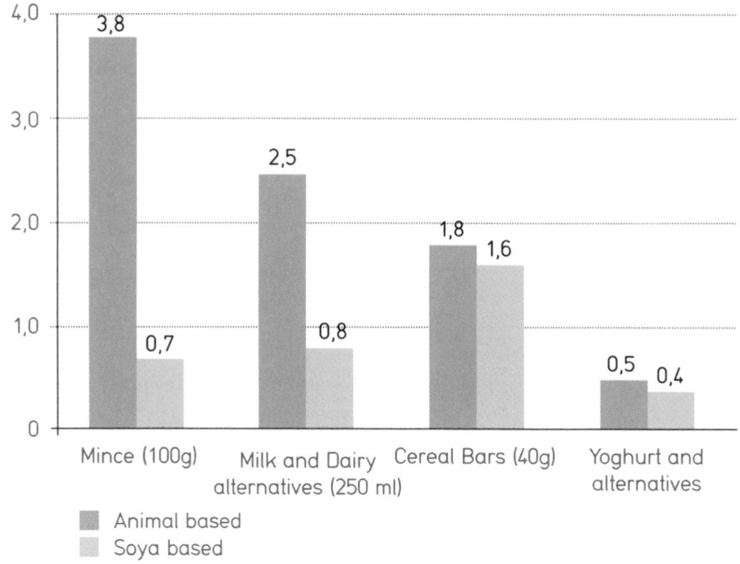

Mince – Very Lean Minced Meat* vs Realeat VegeMince; Semi-skimmed milk* vs Provamel Soya Fresh; Cereal Bar* vs M&S Apricot & Date Cereal Bars; Low fat Dairy Yoghurt* vs Provamel Peach Yofu alternative to yoghurt

* Compeat 5.0 Nutritional analysis system based on the 5th edition of "McCance and Widdowsons The Composition of Foods"

Additional Nutritional Benefits of Plant Foods

The wide array of nutrients found in plant foods (Table 2.2) are also thought to contribute to the potential health benefits associated with plant-based eating.

TABLE 2.2 – Plant-based Food Groups and the Nutrients They Provide

Food Groups	Food Examples	Examples of Nutrients
Whole-grains	Wholemeal bread, whole-grain breakfast cereal, oats, brown rice, wholemeal pasta, popcorn, whole-grain rice cakes, rye crisp breads, oatcakes	Fibre, carbohydrate, protein, B Vitamins, Vitamin E, iron, zinc, copper, selenium, phytonutrients, magnesium, phosphorus, calcium
Legumes including Soya Soya products	Beans such as kidney beans, black eyed beans, baked beans, soya beans and edamame beans. Peas, chickpeas and lentils. Soya products e.g. fortified soya drink, soya alternative to yoghurts and desserts, tofu, meat variations (soya burgers, soya mince),	Protein, carbohydrates, fibre, B vitamins, iron, calcium, zinc and magnesium
Vegetables	Fresh vegetables, salad vegetables, tinned vegetables, frozen vegetables	Folate, calcium, Vitamin A (Beta-Carotene), Vitamin C, fibre, iron, potassium, phytonutrients
Fruits	Fresh fruit, fruit juice, dried fruit, fruit smoothies, tinned fruit in natural juices, frozen fruit	As for vegetables
Nuts and Seeds	Almonds, peanuts, walnuts, cashews, sunflower seeds, pumpkin seeds, linseeds, flaxseeds, peanut butter, tahini	Protein, carbohydrate, fibre, unsaturated fatty acids, zinc, Vitamin E, calcium

Specific attention should be given to the fibre content of these foods (both soluble and insoluble fibre) as currently the intake of fibre in many European countries is below the recommended amounts (see Chapter 01). Including more of these fibre rich foods can help to meet these dietary recommendations.

In addition to nutrients, plant foods also contain other compounds, called phytonutrients. Although not nutrients in the traditional sense, they are found in a variety of different plants and include substances such as phytosterols, lignans, flavonoids, glucosinolates, phenols, terpenes and allium compounds. Research is suggesting that when these are eaten as part of the food (rather than an isolated supplement), these compounds may offer health benefits[14].

Are There Any Nutritional Concerns to Consider when Adopting a Plant-Based Eating Pattern?

No, not if a wide variety of foods is included in the diet to ensure that it's nutritionally balanced. In fact, in their position paper on this issue, the American Dietetic Association (ADA) has said that appropriately planned vegetarian diets are healthful, nutritionally adequate, and may provide health benefits in the prevention and treatment of certain diseases[1].

In the past, there was concern that moving towards a plant-based eating regime would result in deficiencies in particular nutrients, specifically protein, zinc, iron, Vitamin B12, Vitamin D and calcium[8,15,16]. However a review that considered the evidence for this concluded that this needn't be the case and suggested that based on the evidence, meat is an optional rather than an essential constituent of human diets[17].

In developed countries vegetarians often consume a wider variety of foods than meat-eaters and are more likely to eat unrefined carbohydrate foods, salads, fruit, pulses and nuts on a regular basis. As a result the intakes of several nutrients, including thiamin, folate, Vitamin C, carotene, potassium and vitamin E, are higher among vegetarians than in the general population. Although studies have found that protein intake is slightly lower in vegetarians than meat eaters, it is still adequate. While iron and Vitamin B12 are the most likely nutrients to be lacking in these diets, these shouldn't be an issue if the diet is well planned and therefore balanced. In fact in one Australian study, iron intakes were similar in both omnivores and vegetarians (9.9mg and 10.7mg/ day, respectively)[5]. The potential risk of nutritional inadequacy depends on the extent to which animal products are being reduced and plant foods being increased in the diet. Plant-based eating spans a wide spectrum of dietary practices; from vegan diets (where all animal products are excluded) to diets where small amounts of meat are included. Data from the previously mentioned CSFII study found that the vegetarians who ate some meat had significantly higher intakes of omega-3 fatty acids and calcium compared to the non-vegetarians. The percentage of calories coming from protein was similar in both groups and iron intake was slightly higher in the vegetarian group who ate meat, although this was not statistically significant. Vitamin B_{12} and Zinc intakes were slightly lower in this group compared to the non-vegetarian group, but again this was not significant[4]. This highlights that adopting a plant-based eating pattern does not necessarily result in lower intakes of nutrients that are supposedly thought to be at risk when cutting down on animal foods.

However it's important to consider the nutrients animal products generally provide when reducing these in the diet and how best they can be replaced with suitable plant alternatives. For example, meat, eggs and dairy products provide protein, zinc, iron, Vitamin B_{12}, Vitamin D and calcium. Fish is also a good source of long-chain omega-3 fatty acids. Nevertheless these can be replaced. Table 2.3 highlights good alternative plant sources for these particular nutrients.

TABLE 2.3 – Nutritional Contribution from Animal Foods Compared to Plant Foods

Animal Foods	Plant Foods
Protein	Peas, beans, lentils, nuts, nut butters (peanut butter), seeds, soya dairy alternatives (soya drink, soya yoghurts), tofu, soya nuts, meat analogs such as soya mince
Zinc	Beans, lentils, nuts, seeds and whole-grains
Iron	Beans, lentils, peas, nuts, sesame seeds, dried fruit, whole-grains, fortified breakfast cereals, leafy green vegetables
Vitamin B12	Yeast extract and other fortified foods such as soya drink, soya alternative to yoghurts and desserts, breakfast cereals (check the label)
Calcium	Fortified soya dairy alternatives, tofu, dried fruit (e.g. apricots and figs), nuts, green leafy vegetables (especially Kale and Pak-Choi, but not spinach), sesame seeds and tahini
Vitamin D	Fortified foods such as margarines, soya dairy alternatives, some breakfast cereals (check the labels)
Omega-3 fats	Flaxseed, rapeseed, hemp seeds, walnuts, green leafy vegetables and soya oil

A Special Word

Protein

While protein from animal sources contains the complete mix of essential amino acids, most plant foods contain limited amounts of one or more of the essential amino acids. It was once thought that certain combinations of plant foods had to be eaten at the same meal to ensure a sufficient intake of amino acids. However it is now known that as long as energy intake is adequate and a mixture of plant proteins are eaten over the course of the day, the requirement for essential amino acids will be met.

Using the internationally recognised method to determine protein quality (Protein Digestibility Corrected Amino Acid Score (PDCAAS))[18] soya has been identified as one of the few plant foods that contain all the essential amino acids in amounts the body requires. For this reason the quality of soya protein is comparable to meat, milk and eggs.

Iron

Nonhaem iron is present in plant foods and haem iron is found in animal foods. Nonhaem iron is not as well absorbed by the body but its availability is enhanced by the presence of Vitamin C and factors found in meat, fish and eggs. Absorption is also regulated by requirements – lower body stores result in an increased absorption of nonhaem iron. Dietary factors that may inhibit nonhaem iron include phytic acid found in whole-grains and legumes and phenolic compounds found in tea and coffee. Some food preparation techniques such as soaking and sprouting beans, grains and seeds can reduce phytate levels and thereby enhance nonhaem iron absorption. Furthermore as people move towards a plant-based diet they are likely to consume more Vitamin C, which can help overcome these inhibitors of iron absorption.

Interestingly, soya contains a form of iron that is easily absorbed despite the presence of phytate. Although soya is good source of iron, in the past it was believed that this iron, like iron from other plant foods, was poorly available. However research using improved methodologies suggests that iron absorption maybe higher than previously thought because most of the iron in soya is in the form of ferritin[19,20].

In Western societies incidence of iron deficiency anaemia among vegetarians is similar to that of non-vegetarians, although iron stores are often lower[21].
To determine the role meat has in iron and health, a comprehensive review was undertaken by the UK's Scientific Advisory Committee on Nutrition (SACN)[22]. They suggested that a healthy balanced diet, including a variety of foods containing iron, is more important in helping people to achieve adequate iron status than focusing on inhibitors and enhancers of iron from foods.

Vitamin B_{12}

If small amounts of animal foods are included in the diet then getting enough Vitamin B12 shouldn't be a problem. However if all animal products are being excluded it's important to ensure that fortified food sources are included.

Vitamin D

In Western Societies although the action of sunlight on the skin can synthesise Vitamin D during the spring and summer months, at other times of the year it's important to eat foods that contain Vitamin D.

Omega-3 fats

Fish is the major source of the long chain omega-3 fatty acids (docosahexaenoic acid (DHA) and eicosapentaenoic acid (EPA)) while the short version (Alpha Linolenic Acid (ALA)) is found in vegetable oils - particularly flaxseed, walnut and rapeseed oils. The long chain omega-3 fatty acids are particularly important for the maintenance of health, specifically heart health, and many dietary recommendations advise incorporating fish into the diet to meet the requirement for omega-3s. The shorter omega-3 fatty acids may not have the same benefits and although the body can convert some ALA into EPA and DHA, the conversion is believed to be limited. If fish is totally excluded from the diet there could be a risk of low or inadequate omega-3 fatty acid status. Despite this, a recent study has confirmed findings from other studies which have found that although non-fish eating meat eaters and vegetarians have much lower intakes of EPA and DHA than fish eaters, their omega-3 status is higher than would be expected. This suggests a greater conversion of ALA to circulating long chain omega-3 fatty acids in non-fish eating groups[23]. Nevertheless, for those who are not eating any fish and are concerned about getting enough long chain omega-3 fatty acids in their diets there are now supplements made from algae derived DHA.

Eating more plant-based foods, and replacing some animal products with these, can help to improve the nutritional quality of the diet to meet current dietary recommendations.

Plant-based eating supports normal growth and development and can meet the nutritional needs of a healthy individual throughout the lifecycle provided a wide variety of plant foods are consumed.

Animal foods should be seen as an accompaniment, rather than as an essential component of the diet.

The wide variety of plant foods available provides a number of options for designing a healthy plant-based eating plan to suit all tastes and palettes.

Literature chapter 02

1. Craig, W.J. and A.R. Mangels, Position of the American Dietetic Association: vegetarian diets. J Am Diet Assoc, 2009. **109**(7): p. 1266-82.

2. Davey, G.K., et al., EPIC-Oxford: lifestyle characteristics and nutrient intakes in a cohort of 33 883 meat-eaters and 31 546 non meat-eaters in the UK. Public Health Nutr, 2003. **6**(3): p. 259-69.

3. Robinson-O'Brien, R., et al., Adolescent and young adult vegetarianism: better dietary intake and weight outcomes but increased risk of disordered eating behaviors. J Am Diet Assoc, 2009. **109**(4): p. 648-55.

4. Haddad, E.H. and J.S. Tanzman, What do vegetarians in the United States eat? Am J Clin Nutr, 2003. **78**(3 Suppl): p. 626S-632S.

5. Ball, M.J. and M.A. Bartlett, Dietary intake and iron status of Australian vegetarian women. Am J Clin Nutr, 1999. **70**(3): p. 353-8.

6. Nakamoto, K., et al., Nutritional characteristics of middle-aged Japanese vegetarians. J Atheroscler Thromb, 2008. **15**(3): p. 122-9.

7. Alexander, D., M.J. Ball, and J. Mann, Nutrient intake and haematological status of vegetarians and age-sex matched omnivores. Eur J Clin Nutr, 1994. **48**(8): p. 538-46.

8. Draper, A., et al., The energy and nutrient intakes of different types of vegetarian: a case for supplements? Br J Nutr, 1993. **69**(1): p. 3-19.

9. Barr, S.I. and T.M. Broughton, Relative weight, weight loss efforts and nutrient intakes among health-conscious vegetarian, past vegetarian and nonvegetarian women ages 18 to 50. J Am Coll Nutr, 2000. **19**(6): p. 781-8.

10. Janelle, K.C. and S.I. Barr, Nutrient intakes and eating behavior scores of vegetarian and nonvegetarian women. J Am Diet Assoc, 1995. **95**(2): p. 180-6, 189, quiz 187-8.

11. Barr, S.I. and G.E. Chapman, Perceptions and practices of self-defined current vegetarian, former vegetarian, and nonvegetarian women. J Am Diet Assoc, 2002. **102**(3): p. 354-60.

12. Cade, J.E., V.J. Burley, and D.C. Greenwood, The UK Women's Cohort Study: comparison of vegetarians, fish-eaters and meat-eaters. Public Health Nutr, 2004. **7**(7): p. 871-8.

13. Jenkins, D.J., et al., Soy protein reduces serum cholesterol by both intrinsic and food displacement mechanisms. J Nutr, 2010. **140**(12): p. 2302S-2311S.

14. Craig, W. and L. Beck, Phytochemicals: Health Protective Effects. Can J Diet Pract Res, 1999. **60**(2): p. 78-84.

15. Freeland-Graves, J., Mineral adequacy of vegetarian diets. Am J Clin Nutr, 1988. **48**(3 Suppl): p. 859-62.

16. Dwyer, J.T., Nutritional consequences of vegetarianism. Annu Rev Nutr, 1991. **11**: p. 61-91.

17. Sanders, T.A., The nutritional adequacy of plant-based diets. Proc Nutr Soc, 1999. **58**(2): p. 265-9.

18. FAO/WHO Expert Consultation, Protein Quality Evaluation: Food and Agriculture Organization of the United Nations, FAO Food and Nutrition Paper No. 51. Rome, Italy: Food and Agriculture Organization. 1991.

19. Murray-Kolb, L.E., et al., Women with low iron stores absorb iron from soybeans. Am J Clin Nutr, 2003. **77**(1): p. 180-4.

20. Lonnerdal, B., et al., Iron absorption from soybean ferritin in nonanemic women. Am J Clin Nutr, 2006. **83**(1): p. 103-7.

21. Hunt, J.R., Moving toward a plant-based diet: are iron and zinc at risk? Nutr Rev, 2002. **60**(5 Pt 1): p. 127-34.

22. Scientific Advisory Committee on Nutrition. SACN report on iron and health. 2010 February 2011]; Available from: *http://www.sacn.gov.uk/pdfs/sacn_iron_and_health_report_web.pdf.*

23. *Welch, A.A., et al., Dietary intake and status of n-3 polyunsaturated fatty acids in a population of fish-eating and non-fish-eating meat-eaters, vegetarians, and vegans and the precursor-product ratio of alpha-linolenic acid to long-chain n-3 polyunsaturated fatty acids: results from the EPIC-Norfolk cohort. Am J Clin Nutr, 2010.* ***92**(5): p. 1040-51.*

03

Chapter 03

Plant-Based Eating and Health

Summary

Plant-based foods, or eating regimes, have a number of characteristics which may contribute to their role in a healthy lifestyle, these are:

- Both plant-based foods and eating patterns tend to be lower in fat, specifically saturated fat, and have a better unsaturated: saturated fat ratio which is a core recommendation in healthy eating advice, especially related to heart health.
- Both plant-based foods and diets generally have a higher fibre content. This can lower the energy density in the diet, resulting in a lower calorie diet which is beneficial for weight maintenance. The inclusion of some fibre-rich plant foods can also specifically reduce certain risk factors that promote health and well being.
- Specific plant foods or ingredients such as soya, nuts, oat/barley beta glucan have been shown to reduce blood cholesterol and to play an important role in a cholesterol-friendly diet and may also provide other health benefits.
- Many plant-based foods contain compounds called polyphenols, which may act as antioxidants, reducing oxidative damage to lipids, proteins and cells that are key steps in the development of chronic diseases such as cancer. They may also help maintain heart health by reducing the oxidation of the cholesterol in blood and maintaining functionality of the endothelial cells that line the entire circulatory system, from the heart to the smallest capillary. Furthermore, polyphenol components such as isoflavones, flavonols and flavones may inhibit the undesirable platelet aggregation associated with clot formation in the blood and reduce inflammation[1].
- Plant-based foods are typically rich sources of minerals that are essential nutrients and are also co-factors - working alongside the many enzymes which are vital in keeping body cells healthy.
- Many plant-based foods are rich sources of vitamins C, E and carotenes, which among other essential roles, are valuable antioxidant nutrients.
- Some plant-based foods contain biologically active substances, such as plant stanols and sterols, which reduce blood cholesterol.

Potential Health Benefits of Plant-Based Eating

It's likely that it's a combination of all these factors, rather than one specific nutrient, that's responsible for the potential health benefits enjoyed by those who predominately eat plant-based foods. As we progress through the various aspects of health the importance of some of these specific aspects will be discussed.

Introduction to the Science

There are a number of general principles that have been adopted in reviewing the scientific evidence relating to plant-based eating and health. To identify the scientific evidence, initially a search of the scientific literature was undertaken in Medline using the term "plant-based"; this database was supplemented by using the search term "vegetarian" and by hand searching the reference lists in reviews and meta analyses. Animal studies were excluded. A database was established that contained human studies or reviews and that amounted to approximately 900 references. This database was then further searched using terms relevant to each chapter, for example, for the heart health chapter, the additional search terms were "heart", "CVD", "CHD" and "cholesterol". Once the total database had been further searched with terms appropriate to each health condition, sub groups of references were available and these formed the core scientific evidence reviewed for each individual chapter.

The primary sources of information required were studies conducted in humans with plant-based eating patterns. However, in some cases data from vegetarian studies or studies undertaken in those adopting a Mediterranean Diet have been included, as the research in these areas is more extensive and can further add to our understanding of plant-eating.

Scientific support can be obtained from two main sources. Firstly evidence of an association between plant-based eating and subsequent incidence or death from a specific disease. This is provided by observational studies. Broadly speaking, such studies follow a defined group of people for a number of years and relate dietary intake at time intervals, to incidence or death from that specific disease. These are known as cohort or prospective cohort studies. In some cases a cohort study may follow a population for a number of years and measure risk factors of the disease rather than the disease itself. Alternatively data may be collected from a group of people at one time point. Dietary intake characteristics are then divided into a number of sub groups, for example intake of plant foods is divided into thirds (tertiles), fourths (quartiles), fifths (quintiles) etc and then related to markers of disease, such as blood cholesterol or blood pressure in the case of CVD. These are known as longitudinal studies. A third type of observational study is where dietary information is collected from a group of people suffering from a disease and this is compared to a matched group of healthy people, for example of a similar age, gender etc; these are case-controlled studies. Evidence provided by observational studies is reporting an association between factors, not cause and effect.

The second source of evidence is provided by clinical studies in which an intervention takes place. For example, volunteers are introduced to a plant-based diet and the effect which this change has on markers of CVD is measured. By use of a control or placebo group, it is possible to specifically measure the effect of such an intervention and, "cause and effect" can be established. Such studies may often be randomised controlled trials (RCTs). The gold standard in RCTs is where both the volunteers and the researchers are blinded (do not have knowledge of which treatment or control group they are undertaking, or observing in the case of the researchers); these are referred to as double-blinded RCTs. However in the area of nutrition, few studies are double-blinded as it is obvious when a change to the diet is made, especially if a new food is introduced. Nevertheless there are some very high quality nutrition-related RCTs in the literature.

Evidence provided by both groups of studies is valuable; observational studies tend to be much longer term and provide information about the health impact of adopting a particular lifestyle and also provide feedback on day to day practice. The shorter duration clinical studies provide an insight into the change in specific risk factors by, say, changing the eating pattern. Clinical studies may also help develop an understanding of the mechanisms involved and why a particular intervention is effective. The evidence provided by well-designed and conducted clinical studies is considered by such authorities as EFSA (European Food Safety Authority) to be of the highest standard. Often scientists will take either a group of clinical studies, or observational studies, conducted on the same topic and in a similar manner, and pool the findings to assess how convincing the evidence is in the whole area of study. This statistical analysis is known as a meta analysis and helps to weigh the totality of the evidence. Meta analyses, carried out with clinical trials, which have significant positive outcomes, are considered highly convincing evidence.

In the following chapters, information from both clinical and observational studies is detailed, providing an insight into the overall strength of the evidence for the potential health benefits of plant-based eating.

Plant-based foods and eating patterns are typically low in saturated fat, and high in unsaturated fats and fibre. This is important in maintaining healthy blood cholesterol levels and a healthy body weight.

Eating more fruit, vegetables, legumes, whole-grains, nuts and seeds that contain biologically active substances such as beta glucans and plant stanols or sterols is a simple and easy way to look after the heart.

In addition, specific components found intrinsically in plant foods including minerals, vitamins and antioxidants may work together to bring further health benefits.

An increasing database of good quality scientific studies demonstrate that plant-based eating is associated with improved health and well being.

Literature chapter 03

1. Rao, V. and A. Al-Weshahy, Plant-based diets and control of lipids and coronary heart disease risk. Curr Atheroscler Rep, 2008. 10(6): p. 478-85.

04

Chapter 04

Plant-Based Eating and Cardiovascular Health

Summary

- Heart disease and stroke together are the most important cause of death in Europe.
- Evidence from observational studies indicates that typically the incidence of heart disease is around 20% lower in those following a plant-based eating pattern.
- Plant-based eating is associated with a healthier blood cholesterol profile, specifically lower LDL cholesterol.
- Results from two well-conducted clinical trials suggest that plant-based eating can lower total and LDL cholesterol by 8-10% and 9-15% respectively.
- There is limited evidence suggesting that blood pressure may also be lower in those following a plant-based eating regime.
- Studies indicate that people consuming more plant foods tend to have a lower saturated fat intake and this may be one of the reasons that LDL-cholesterol is lowered, but there are a variety of other factors intrinsic to plant-based eating which may also be important.
- Overall, plant-based eating promotes heart health and should be recommended in dietary advice to support a healthy heart.

Incidence of Cardiovascular Disease in Europe

Coronary heart disease (CHD) and stroke together are known as Cardiovascular disease (CVD). It is the single most important cause of death in Europe and causes 4.3 million deaths per year, representing 48% of all deaths. CVD is the most important cause of death in women and the most important in men except in France, The Netherlands and Spain[1].

Heart disease leads to over 1.9 million deaths in the European Union. One of the most important modifiable risk factors is raised blood cholesterol[2]. The World Health Organisation (WHO) estimates that over 60% of CHD and 40% of stroke in developed countries is due to total blood cholesterol levels in excess of the theoretical minimum, 3.8mmol/L[2]. This is further confirmed by reference to the INTERHEART case controlled study, which identified that 45% of heart attacks in Western Europe and 35% in Central and Eastern Europe were due to abnormal blood lipids. Those with abnormal blood lipids have a three-fold greater risk of heart attack compared to those with normal levels[3]. Death from CVD is higher in men than women, although women's risk of CVD increases after the menopause and is also markedly higher in Eastern Europe compared to Western Europe (see Figure 4.1).

FIGURE 4.1 – Estimated Age Standardized Death Rate (per 100,000) from Cardiovascular Disease in 4 Western and 2 Eastern European Countries

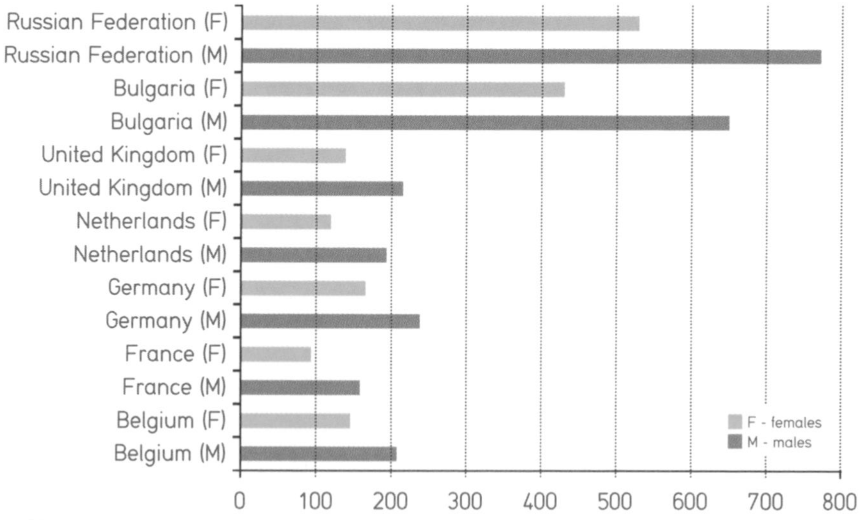

Source: WHO, CVD statistics

Risk Factors for Cardiovascular Disease

Risk factors for heart disease include high blood cholesterol, high blood pressure (BP), type 2 diabetes, overweight and obesity. These are factors that can be controlled by the individual to some degree. There are also a number of risk factors for CVD that are outside of an individual's direct control, such as age, gender, ethnicity and family history of the disease.

The most important behavioural risk factors are unhealthy diet, physical inactivity and tobacco use. Together these behavioural risk factors are responsible for about 80% of CHD and stroke.

Heart disease doesn't have a single cause, generally it is a combination of factors, which increase in severity over time, leading to a heart attack or stroke. The behavioural risk factors, physical inactivity or smoking tobacco, are easily identifiable and lifestyle change can readily be undertaken to moderate these risks. For example, simply being more active and giving up smoking. However, defining healthy eating and putting it into practice has proved to be more difficult. In the past emphasis was placed on the nutrient profile of heart-healthy diets, for example, advice was given to reduce fat, particularly saturated fat intake, and to increase fibre intake. It is now recognised that food-based recommendations are more useful and lead to better uptake and results[4]. For most of the common disorders and diseases including CVD, obesity, type 2 diabetes and many cancers, diets that are rich in fruits and vegetables have been associated with lower risk[5]. Consequently recent recommendations focus on the increased consumption of plant-based foods (see Introduction). Important sources of plant food are fruits, vegetables, legumes, whole-grain cereals, nuts and seeds.

Scientific evidence evaluating the benefits of plant-based eating and heart health is steadily accumulating. However defining and quantifying the exact amount of plant foods consumed is problematical and inexact, with the result that data is drawn from a variety of diets in order to establish the extent to which an association exists. For example, information has been taken from eating practices referred to as vegetarian, semi-vegetarian, lacto-ovo vegetarian and primary plant-based diets (essentially lacto-ovo vegetarian diet with small amounts of meat or fish).

The risk factors for heart disease that are frequently measured in studies are blood lipids, specifically low density lipoprotein cholesterol (LDL-C) – the so-called – "bad cholesterol", high density lipoprotein (HDL-C) – "good cholesterol", total cholesterol (TC), triglycerides (TAG) and blood pressure (BP). With the exception of HDL-C, elevated levels of these are undesirable. Disruption of endothelial cells that line the entire circulatory system, from the heart to the smallest capillary, is an early indication of heart disease and inflammation has been shown to contribute to this. Consequently many clinical studies will measure endothelial function by using a flow-mediated dilatation (FMD) technique. This measures the blood flow through a specific blood vessel - basically the faster the flow, the better. Changes in inflammatory and endothelial markers or molecules associated with adhesion and clot formation, such as C-reactive protein (CRP), human interleukin-6 (IL-6), human E-selectin, human intercellular adhesion molecule-1 (ICAM) and vascular cell adhesion molecule (VCAM) may also be used to assess coronary health. The next stage in the development of CVD is the development of a thrombosis when a large clot forms in the blood vessel. If this clot stops the blood supply from reaching the heart, it leads to a heart attack. Or alternatively, should it prevent blood from reaching the brain, this leads to a stroke. Blood clots form when cells in the blood called platelets stick together (platelet aggregation) and this measurement may also be used to assess CVD risk. Overweight and obesity, and type 2 diabetes are independent risk factors for CVD, as well as a source of poor health in their own right; information relating to them can be found in Chapters 05 & 06 respectively.

Potential Benefits of Plant-based Eating

Plant-based foods or eating patterns have a number of characteristics which may contribute to their role in heart health. Specifically these are low in saturated fat, high in fibre (often soluble fibres that have been shown to reduce blood cholesterol) and rich sources of antioxidants and micronutrients. In addition, specific plant foods or components have been shown to reduce blood cholesterol and to play an important role in a cholesterol-friendly diet, for example soya protein, almonds, oat/barley beta glucan and plant stanols and sterols.

Observational Studies

The CVD observational studies fall into two distinct groups. One group measures the number of cardiac events or death from CVD and are considered more convincing evidence because they measure a specific event. Whereas the second group measures risk factors such as cholesterol or BP which provide an indication of heart health status.

Much of this data comes from studies where subjects have been following vegetarian or semi-vegetarian diets. For example, results from five prospective cohort studies were combined to compare the death rates from common diseases of vegetarians, with those of non vegetarians with similar lifestyles. In this sample of 76,172 men and women aged 16–89 years, there were 8,330 deaths after an average follow-up period of 10.6 years. Death from heart disease was almost a quarter lower in vegetarians, than in non vegetarians. This was reported as a death rate ratio (DRR) of 0.76 and was statistically significant ($P < 0.01$). This effect was more pronounced in those who had followed a vegetarian diet from a younger age and for more than 5 years. There was also a 7% lower death rate from stroke in the vegetarian populations, although this was not significant[6].

Two of the previously mentioned prospective studies were based on UK populations – the Healthy Food Shoppers Study and the Oxford Vegetarian Study. These have now been added to by a third, more recent, study – the European Prospective Investigation into Cancer Nutrition-Oxford (EPIC-Oxford) cohort which includes data from approximately 56,000 subjects. Together these three studies provide an insight into plant-based eating in the UK. Within each study it is possible to compare vegetarians with non vegetarians and the resulting DRRs for heart disease, adjusted for age, sex and smoking, were 0.85 in the Health Food Shoppers Study, 0.86 in the Oxford Vegetarian Study, and 0.75 in EPIC-Oxford. The authors concluded that overall mortality of both the vegetarians and the non vegetarians in these studies was low compared with national rates. However the non significant reduction in mortality from heart disease was in line with previous findings, at just under 20%[7]. This data was confirmed in a recent update from EPIC-Oxford published in 2009. On this occasion when vegetarians were compared to meat eaters (47,254 subjects), who had no previous history of cardiovascular disease or cancer, the adjusted risk factor for heart disease was 0.81 representing a reduced risk of 19%[8].

A plant-based eating regime that did not exclude all animal products was assessed by comparing dietary patterns using data from the USA, specifically from the Nurse's Health Study[9]. Consumption of a diet that was high in fruit and vegetables, whole-grains, fish and poultry, and low-fat dairy products, a so-called "prudent diet", was compared to a typical Western-style diet. This prudent diet was associated with a significantly reduced risk of heart disease compared to the Western-style diet. The relative risk (RR) of death from heart disease was 36% lower, (RR 0.64) for those consuming the highest proportion of fruit, vegetables, whole-grains and fish in their diet[9]. In a similar analysis, the RRs of stroke was established; those consuming the highest proportion of components that made up the prudent diet had a 22% reduced risk of developing stroke compared to the Western diet[10].

A Mediterranean diet is another example of a plant-rich eating pattern that can be used to help understand the relationship with heart disease. In a study that assessed CHD events in five Spanish centres of the EPIC study, compliance to a Mediterranean diet was assessed relative to CHD[11]. The extent to which a Mediterranean diet was followed was based on the intake of nine key components and an overall 18-point score developed. Six components: fruit, (including nuts and seeds but excluding fruit juices), vegetables (excluding potatoes), legumes, cereals (including whole-grain and refined flour, pasta, rice, other grains, and bread), fresh fish (including seafood) and olive oil were viewed positively and two components viewed negatively, these were total meat (including processed meat) and dairy products. Alcohol was considered beneficial in moderation. The analysis included 41,078 participants aged 29-69 years, recruited in 1992-1996. They were then followed up for an average period of 10.4 years. Fatal and nonfatal CHD events were analyzed according to subjects' Mediterranean dietary score. A high compliance to the Mediterranean diet was associated with a 40% significant reduction in risk of heart disease compared to low compliance. It was calculated that a 1-unit increase in relative Mediterranean diet score was associated with a 6% reduced risk of CHD, implying that following a regime based on plant foods and fish was associated with significantly improved heart health in Spain.

While this dataset of observational studies is not a perfect match for plant-based eating, there is consistency in the findings, indicating that those who consume more plants foods and less or no meat tend to have improved heart health and a lower death rate from heart disease and possibly stroke.

An extensive review of plant-based diets and their effect on the risk factor - blood lipids - has recently been undertaken by Ferdowsian[12]. In this review, the authors identified 13 observational studies with a total of 4772 men and women of varying age and ethnicity, and who were from six different countries, including the UK and Germany. In 12 of the 13 identified studies, blood cholesterol levels were lower in those adopting plant-based eating. The authors concluded that those following a plant-based diet, particularly vegetarian and vegan diets had lower cholesterol concentrations and were at lower risk of heart disease. Within this systematic review of studies there were four studies that related to Seventh-Day Adventists populations, who have very different lifestyles to many Western populations. Therefore care should be taken interpreting this data and its applicability to the general population. Of greater interest within this review are those studies that compared sub populations such as vegans, vegetarians, semi-vegetarians (or fish eating vegetarians) to meat eaters. For example, in the single largest study, which was conducted in 3,277 UK subjects, it was found that TC and LDL-C were higher in meat eaters than vegans, with vegetarians and fish eaters having intermediate and similar values[13].

Clinical Studies

The recent review of Ferdowsian also included data from RCTs that specifically measured the effect of plant-based eating on blood lipids. Of these, there are two good quality studies, the first of which evaluated two low fat diets. In this study, the diets were designed to be identical in total fat, saturated fat, protein, carbohydrate, and cholesterol content, consistent with the former American Heart Association Step I guidelines of 30% of energy (e) or less from total fat and 10% or less from saturated fat. The control "Low-Fat" diet contained foods relatively typical of a low-fat U.S. diet and the "Low-Fat Plus" diet incorporated considerably more vegetables, legumes, and whole-grains[14]. The study was of 4 weeks duration and conducted in 120 adults aged 30 to 65 years of age, with initial LDL-C concentrations of 3.3 to 4.8 mmol/L (mildly elevated) and who were either normal weight, or overweight, but not obese. Blood lipid concentrations were measured at baseline and at the end of the study. A 7-day menu cycle was developed for the participants who consumed lunch or dinner on site at the University of Stanford's Research Center dining facility. Those in the Low-Fat Plus group, on average, consumed per day more fruit (0.8 servings), vegetables (7.6 servings), beans, legumes, nuts and seeds (3.7 servings) and whole-grains (3.5 servings) and less refined grains (2.5 servings), dairy products (0.1 servings) and meat, fish and eggs (1.1 servings).

The 4-week changes in blood lipids from baseline are given in Figure 4.2. The reduction in TC and LDL-C were significantly greater in the Low-Fat Plus diet ($P < 0.02$); respective values for the Low-Fat and Low-Fat Plus were -0.24mmol/L and -0.46mmol/L for TC and -0.18mmol/L and -0.36mmol/L for LDL-C. The percentage reduction in blood lipids in the Low-Fat Plus diet compared to baseline was 8% and 9% respectively for TC and LDL-C. The effects on HDL-C and blood triglycerides (TAG) were similar between the groups and little changed compared to baseline.

The authors concluded that emphasis on including nutrient-dense plant-based foods, consistent with recently revised national guidelines, increased the total and LDL cholesterol–lowering effect of a low-fat diet.

FIGURE 4.2 – The Mean Change in Plasma Lipids after Following a Low Fat Diet

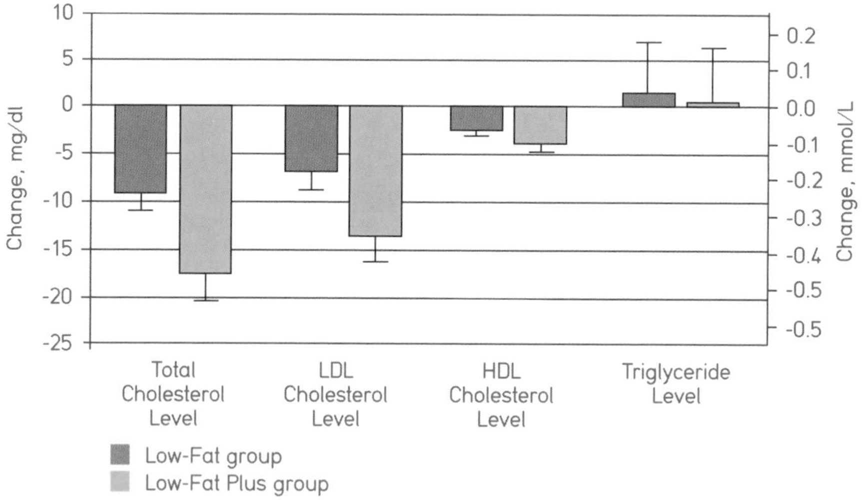

Source: Gardner, C.D., et al., Ann Intern Med, 2005. **142**(9): p. 725-33.

In the second identified RCT, the Optimal Macronutrient Intake Trial to Prevent Heart Disease (Omni-Heart) was a 3-period crossover design[15]. Two clinical centres (Johns Hopkins Medical Institutions and Brigham and Women's Hospital) conducted the trial. Three healthful diets, each with reduced saturated fat intake (6%e), were evaluated with respect to their effect on BP and blood lipids. The 3 dietary groups were:

- Rich in carbohydrates (CHO), similar to the DASH (Dietary Approaches to Stop Hypertension) diet[16], which emphasises fruits, vegetables and low fat dairy products; total fat 27%e, protein 15%e, carbohydrate 58%e;
- Rich in protein, about half of which was from plant sources (PR); total fat 27%e, protein 25%e (half of which was from plant protein), carbohydrate 48%e;
- Rich in unsaturated fat, predominantly monounsaturated fat (USFA); total fat 37%e (21%e from monounsaturated fat and 10%e PUFA), protein 15%e group, carbohydrate 48%e.

As this was crossover in design, one third of the subjects consumed one of the 3 diets for 6 weeks, followed by a 2 week wash-out period, before crossing over to one of the other 3 diets for 6 weeks. The final diet was consumed after another 2 week wash-out period. The 164 participants were generally healthy men and women, aged 30 years and older, either prehypertensive (systolic BP (SBP), 120-139 mmHg or diastolic BP, (DBP), 80-89 mmHg) or stage 1 hypertensives (SBP, 140-159 mmHg or DBP, 90-99 mmHg). Diet was well-controlled with a 7-day menu cycle developed for each diet. Throughout the study, participants were provided all of their food which was prepared in research kitchens. On each weekday, participants ate their main meal on-site.

Food group targets were also established for each treatment: fruit, vegetables, legumes, nuts, seeds, other vegetable proteins and lean poultry intake were increased in the PR group, with a focus on low fat dairy products.

Data relating to blood lipids and BP was established during the run-in period, at baseline and during the treatment phase at weeks 4-6. The results compared to baseline are shown below in Figures 4.3 and 4.4.

In all groups, both TC and LDL-C was reduced significantly; in the PR group the TC reduction was significantly greater than the CHO and USFA groups (both $P < 0.001$) and represented a reduction of 10% compared to baseline. The reductions for CHO and USFA groups were lower at 6% and 8% respectively. Furthermore there was a significantly greater reduction in LDL-C in the PR group than in the CHO group ($P = 0.01$) and represented a reduction compared to baseline of 15%. There was little effect on HDL. In contrast, there was a marked reduction in TAG in the PR and USFA groups; this reduction in TAG was significantly greater in the PR group compared to the CHO group ($P < 0.001$) and the USFA group ($P = 0.03$).

FIGURE 4.3 – The Mean Change in Plasma Lipids after Following a Low Fat Diet Rich in Either Carbohydrate, Plant Protein and Unsaturated Fat

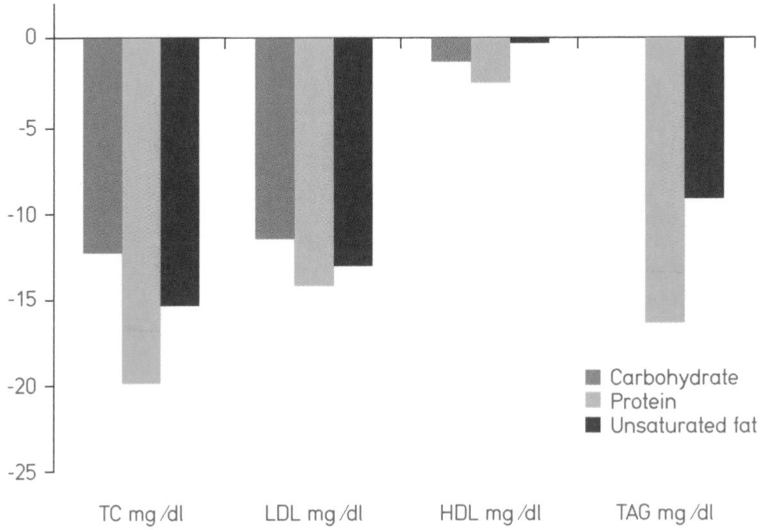

Source data extracted from: Appel, L.J., et al., JAMA, 2005. 294(19): p. 2455-64.

FIGURE 4.4 – The Mean Change in Blood Pressure after Following a Low Fat Diet Rich in Either Carbohydrate, Plant Protein and Unsaturated Fat

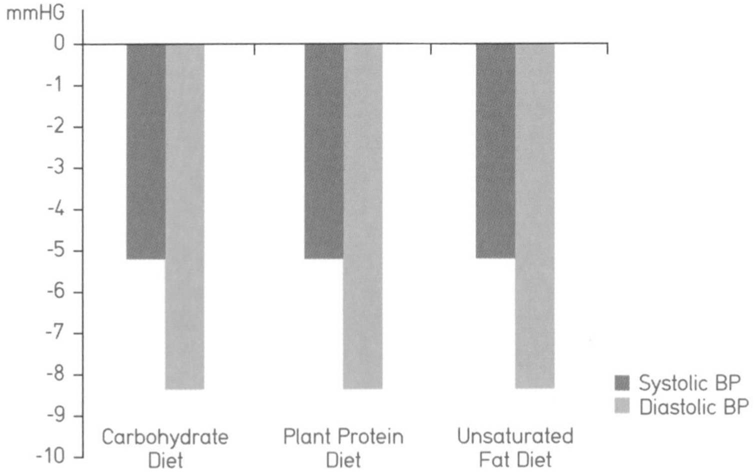

Source data extracted from: Appel, L.J., et al., JAMA, 2005. 294(19): p. 2455-64.

From the BP data in Figure 4.4, it can be seen that BP, both SBP and DBP, were reduced in all groups compared to baseline. There was a greater reduction in SBP and DBP in the PR group compared to the CHO group (P = 0.002 and P < 0.001 respectively), but they were comparable to those in the USFA group. The average reduction in SBP and DBP in the PR group compared to baseline was 7% in both cases. The extent of BP reduction was greater in those suffering from mild hypertension than in the prehypertensive.

These are the only two RCTs that specifically study the effects of plant-based diets in healthy subjects. Both studies are well-conducted and with similar outcomes. In both cases there is a reduction of TC of between 8-10% and a reduction in LDL-C of between 9-15% compared to baseline. These changes are beneficial to heart health. There is little effect on HDL, which was marginally lower in both trials compared to baseline. A point of difference is the effect on TAG, only in the second study was there a significant reduction, possibly due to the lower carbohydrate content in this diet[15].

Portfolio Diets and Blood Lipids

A further group of studies that will be briefly referred to are those conducted by Prof Jenkins and colleagues from the University of Toronto, Canada. They developed the concept of a "portfolio diet". Portfolio diets are low fat diets based on plant foods, specifically those plant foods or ingredients proven to reduce blood cholesterol. Such foods and ingredients include soya protein, viscous fibres and tree nuts that reduce LDL-C by around 0.15-0.25mmol/L (equivalent to around a 3-8% reduction compared to baseline) and plant stanols or sterols, which reduce LDL-C by 0.30-0.35mmol/L (equivalent to a reduction of 7-10.5% compared to control values). Around ten RCTs have been conducted with "portfolio diets" in adults, usually with mildly elevated cholesterol levels. Typically the diets include soya protein at 16-23g/1000kcal, viscous fibres at 9-19g/1000kcal and tree nuts (almonds at 14-17g/1000kcal) and plant sterols at around 1g/1000kcal. The cholesterol-reduction reported in these relatively short-term studies is usually highly statistically significant (P < 0.001), with LDL-C being approximately 20-35% lower than in the control diets[12]. Of interest is a long term portfolio study conducted for a year in a free living population in Toronto, Canada[17]. This study involved 66 volunteers, who over the period of a year, on average, reduced LDL-C by around 13%. Where compliance to the portfolio diet was better, the extent of cholesterol-reduction reported was greater. In around 30% of motivated participants, LDL-cholesterol concentrations were lowered by more than 20%. This was not significantly different from their response to a first-generation statin taken under metabolically controlled conditions[17].

Portfolio Studies Measuring Blood Pressure

Volunteers undertaking portfolio diet studies have also had their BP determined. In the long term portfolio study mentioned previously, the corresponding reductions from baseline in systolic and diastolic BP at 1 year in 66 subjects were -4.2 mmHg (P=0.002) and -2.3 mmHg (P=0.001), respectively[18]. However, in the portfolio studies of shorter duration, the changes in blood pressure are modest, with some studies reporting a significant reduction and others reporting no change. In the case of DBP this difference may be related to a lack of an effect on bodyweight, as weight loss was significantly associated with DBP in the long-term study.

Other Intervention Studies

There are a number of other reports of lacto-ovo vegetarian, vegetarian and vegan RCTs included in the review of Ferdowsian[12], who concluded that primary plant-based and lacto-ovo vegetarian dietary interventions reduce TC by 10% and LDL-C by 15%[12]. The reductions in vegan dietary interventions are in the range 15-25% and those reported for combination dietary interventions (portfolio diets) are 20-35%. The HDL is typically lower in vegetarians compared to non vegetarians, but the effect on TAG levels is less consistent.

There are fewer studies investigating the association between BP and plant-based eating regimes. Although the DASH studies have reported reductions in BP. These studies evaluated the effect of diets rich in vegetables, fruits, and low-fat dairy products in subjects with or without hypertension. For example, a DASH diet with a low sodium intake, resulted in a mean SBP that was 7.1 mm Hg lower in participants without hypertension, and 11.5 mm Hg lower in participants with hypertension[16]. Overall it appears there may be a small beneficial effect, but at this stage the information is not sufficient to quantity the benefit.

Intervention Studies on Other Markers of Heart Disease

Plant-based eating and lifestyle changes have been shown to play a role in the regression of atherosclerosis, improvement of CV risk profiles, and decreased cardiac events in subjects suffering from heart disease[19]. The Multisite Cardiac Lifestyle Intervention Program measured endothelial function and inflammatory markers of atherosclerosis in 27 volunteers with coronary artery disease (CAD) and/or risk factors for CAD. The volunteers were asked to make changes in their diet to achieve a plant-based diet with 10% of calories from fat, participate in moderate exercise (3 hours/week), and practice stress management (1 hour/day). At the baseline endothelium-dependent brachial artery flow-mediated dilatation (FMD) was performed in the control and intervention groups. After 12 weeks, FMD had improved in the experimental group from a baseline of 4.23mm to 4.65mm, compared to the control group where it decreased from 4.62mm to 4.48mm ($P < 0.0001$). Also, significant decreases occurred in C-reactive protein (from 2.07 to 1.6 mg/L, $P = 0.03$) and interleukin-6 (from 2.52 to 1.23 pg/ml, $P = 0.02$) after 12 weeks. The authors concluded that the significant improvement in FMD, C-reactive protein, and interleukin-6 in the experimental group suggests one or more potential mechanisms underlying the clinical CV benefits of plant-based eating.

Overview and Conclusions

Both plant-based foods and eating patterns tend to be lower in fat, specifically saturated fat and have a better monounsaturated: saturated fat ratio. This nutrient profile has been associated with lower blood cholesterol. There is wide acceptance among scientists that one of the important ways that plant-based eating improves heart health is by its action on blood lipids[20]. Prof Jenkins and colleagues recently explored the extent to which the displacement of fatty foods from the diet, with a plant food (soya), was responsible for the cholesterol lowering properties of soya foods. Using data from 11 RCTs, it was calculated that when comparable amounts of animal proteins were replaced with soya proteins there would be a 3.6-6.0% reduction in LDL-C due to the displacement of saturated fats and cholesterol from the diet. This he called the extrinsic effect. Overall the total reported LDL-C reductions for soya protein have been estimated to be between 7.9 to 10.3% and the difference between this total and the extrinsic effect, has been called the intrinsic effect[21]. It is highly likely that plant foods as a whole have a similar extrinsic effect on the diet and part of their beneficial effect on health is related to an overall healthier nutrient composition. However, there are intrinsic benefits of plant foods too. Some of the intrinsic effects may be the result of direct blood lipid-lowering effects, such as seen with soya, almonds, oats, green tea and soluble fibres. Evidence for a role of improved blood lipid profile is also provided by observational studies with vegetarians, or those following a prudent dietary regime[12], and evidence of reduced incidence of CHD from observational studies with vegetarians or a Mediterranean diet.

The significance of reducing blood cholesterol has been expressed in public health terms by the WHO, where it has been suggested that each 1% reduction in LDL-C in the population, could lead to a 2%–4% reduction in CVD[22]. From the two good quality RCTs identified, it can be seen that plant-based eating is associated with a LDL-C reduction of between 9-15%. Using this data as a basis for calculating CVD-risk reduction, this would be equivalent to a decrease in CVD risk of 18- 30%. This extent of risk reduction is confirmed by reference to the observational studies; those following vegetarian or plant-rich prudent eating patterns have been shown have a lower incidence of cardiovascular death of around 20%.

In addition to the effect on blood lipids, there appears to be some evidence of an effect on BP. Blood pressure reduction is significant for public health, where it has been suggested that a 1% reduction in DBP in the UK population could prevent around 1500 deaths from CHD each year. Currently, however, insufficient evidence exists to quantity a benefit in public health terms of plant-based eating. Nevertheless, although definitive information is not available, BP normalisation may be another contributing factor to the improved heart health reported in the observational studies. In addition, with plant-based eating there may be vascular benefits that derive from improved health of the epithelium, but further research is required in this area.

Plant foods intrinsically contain many beneficial compounds that, by acting through multiple mechanisms, provide protection against heart disease. Of these, it is likely that the rich supply of antioxidants found in many plant foods is important. Yet there is controversy as to how well the antioxidant properties of foods relate to their ability to have an antioxidant function in the body. However, whether or not plant foods do act as antioxidants, they do seem to have an important signalling and regulatory functions that enhance cell function[23]. In addition, polyphenol components such as isoflavones, flavonols and flavones may also inhibit platelet aggregation and reduce inflammation[24].

Plant-based eating is associated with a nutrient-rich diet. Of the micronutrients found in plants foods, potassium is important as it tends to displace sodium, which as seen from the DASH diets is beneficial in BP control[16]. Selenium is also present at good levels in certain plant foods, and as well as being a co-factor for enzymes, is strongly associated with antioxidant functions in the cell. Furthermore plant-based diets tend to be higher in fibre. Both soluble and insoluble fibre results in a lower energy density diet and can improve satiety and enhance the feeling of fullness. Not surprisingly, plant-based eating is associated with lower body weight and less weight gain over time. As overweight and obesity are one of the key modifiable risk factors for heart disease, it may be this effect that further contributes to a role in promoting heart health[25].

Good quality scientific studies demonstrate that plant-based eating is associated with a reduced risk of heart disease.

Plant-based foods and eating patterns are typically low in saturated fat, and high in unsaturated fats and fibre. This is important in maintaining healthy blood cholesterol levels and subsequently a healthy heart.

In addition, specific components found intrinsically in plant foods may work together to bring further heart health benefits.

Eating more fruit, vegetables, legumes, whole-grains, nuts and seeds is a simple and easy way to look after the heart.

Literature chapter 04

1. Petersen, S., et al., *European cardiovascular disease statistics.* 2005, London: British Heart Foundation.
2. World Health Organisation, *The World Health Report 2002; Reducing Risks, Promoting Healthy Life.* 2002, WHO: Geneva.
3. Yusuf, S., et al., *Global burden of cardiovascular diseases: Part I: General considerations, the epidemiological transition, risk factors, and impact of urbanization.* Circulation, 2001. **104**: p. 2746 - 2753.
4. WHO, *Preparation and use of food-based dietary guidelines. Joint FAO/WHO Consultation, Nicosia, Cyprus, 1995* in *WHO Technical Report Series 880.* 1995, http://www.who.int/nutrition/publications/nutrientrequirements/WHO_TRS_880/en/index.html.
5. World Health Organization/Food and Agriculture Organization, *Diet, Nutrition and the Prevention of Chronic Diseases*, in *WHO Technical Report Series, no. 916.* 2003, WHO: Geneva.
6. Key, T.J., G.K. Davey, and P.N. Appleby, *Health benefits of a vegetarian diet.* Proc Nutr Soc, 1999. **58**(2): p. 271-5.
7. Key, T.J., et al., *Mortality in British vegetarians: review and preliminary results from EPIC-Oxford.* Am J Clin Nutr, 2003. **78**(3 Suppl): p. 533S-538S.
8. Key, T.J., et al., *Mortality in British vegetarians: results from the European Prospective Investigation into Cancer and Nutrition (EPIC-Oxford).* Am J Clin Nutr, 2009. **89**(5): p. 1613S-1619S.
9. Fung, T.T., et al., *Dietary patterns and the risk of coronary heart disease in women.* Arch Intern Med, 2001. **161**(15): p. 1857-62.
10. Fung, T.T., et al., *Prospective study of major dietary patterns and stroke risk in women.* Stroke, 2004. **35**(9): p. 2014-9.
11. Buckland, G., et al., *Adherence to the Mediterranean diet and risk of coronary heart disease in the Spanish EPIC Cohort Study.* Am J Epidemiol, 2009. **170**(12): p. 1518-29.
12. Ferdowsian, H.R. and N.D. Barnard, *Effects of plant-based diets on plasma lipids.* Am J Cardiol, 2009. **104**(7): p. 947-56.
13. Thorogood, M., et al., *Plasma lipids and lipoprotein cholesterol concentrations in people with different diets in Britain.* Br Med J (Clin Res Ed), 1987. **295**(6594): p. 351-3.
14. Gardner, C.D., et al., *The effect of a plant-based diet on plasma lipids in hypercholesterolemic adults: a randomized trial.* Ann Intern Med, 2005. **142**(9): p. 725-33.
15. Appel, L.J., et al., *Effects of protein, monounsaturated fat, and carbohydrate intake on blood pressure and serum lipids: results of the OmniHeart randomized trial.* JAMA, 2005. **294**(19): p. 2455-64.
16. Sacks, F.M., et al., *Effects on blood pressure of reduced dietary sodium and the Dietary Approaches to Stop Hypertension (DASH) diet. DASH-Sodium Collaborative Research Group.* N Engl J Med, 2001. **344**(1): p. 3-10.
17. Jenkins, D.J., et al., *Assessment of the longer-term effects of a dietary portfolio of cholesterol-lowering foods in hypercholesterolemia.* Am J Clin Nutr, 2006. **83**(3): p. 582-91.
18. Jenkins, D.J., et al., *Long-term effects of a plant-based dietary portfolio of cholesterol-lowering foods on blood pressure.* Eur J Clin Nutr, 2008. **62**(6): p. 781-8.
19. Dod, H.S., et al., *Effect of intensive lifestyle changes on endothelial function and on inflammatory markers of atherosclerosis.* Am J Cardiol, 2010. **105**(3): p. 362-7.
20. Mensink, R.P., et al., *Effects of dietary fatty acids and carbohydrates on the ratio of serum total to HDL cholesterol and on serum lipids and apolipoproteins: a meta-analysis of 60 controlled trials.* Am J Clin Nutr, 2003. **77**(5): p. 1146-55.
21. Jenkins, D.J., et al., *Soy protein reduces serum cholesterol by both intrinsic and food displacement mechanisms.* J Nutr, 2010. **140**(12): p. 2302S-2311S.
22. World Health Organisation, *Gaining health:The European Strategy for the Prevention and Control of Noncommunicable Diseases.* 2006, http://www.euro.who.int/document/E89306.pdf accessed 20/01/09.
23. Benzie, I.F. and S. Wachtel-Galor, *Vegetarian diets and public health: biomarker and redox connections.* Antioxid Redox Signal, 2010. **13**(10): p. 1575-91.
24. Rao, V. and A. Al-Weshahy, *Plant-based diets and control of lipids and coronary heart disease risk.* Curr Atheroscler Rep, 2008. **10**(6): p. 478-85.
25. Jacobs, D.R., Jr., et al., *Food, plant food, and vegetarian diets in the US dietary guidelines: conclusions of an expert panel.* Am J Clin Nutr, 2009. **89**(5): p. 1549S-1552S.

05

Chapter 05

Plant-Based Eating and Weight Control

Summary

- Maintaining a healthy weight is a major public health challenge in Europe.
- Overweight affects 30–80% of adults in the countries of the WHO European Region. About 20% of children and adolescents are overweight, and a third of these are obese.
- WHO guidelines for promoting healthy behaviours to encourage, motivate and enable individuals to lose weight, recommend eating more fruit and vegetables, as well as nuts and whole-grains.
- Evidence from observational studies indicates those who follow plant-based eating, such as vegetarians or a Mediterranean style diet, tend to have a lower body mass index and gain less weight over time.
- Weight-reducing diets based on plant-based foods are as effective as standard weight loss diets and there is some evidence of improved blood lipid profile, thereby reducing heart disease risk.
- Plant-based eating is associated with less energy dense diets that are lower in saturated fat, as well as lifestyle factors that are associated with better weight management.

Challenge of Weight Management in Europe

It is usually the lack of weight management that catches the headlines, with continuing concern about both the number of people that are heavier than the ideal weight range and the ever increasing number of people who are overweight. Such is the concern that Health ministers in Europe have signed a European Charter committing to halt the rise in obesity by 2015[1].

In the World Health Organisation (WHO) European Region, overweight and obesity are recognised as serious public health challenges. In its 2007 report, WHO cited the following facts about European populations body weight[2]:

- Overweight affects 30–80% of adults in the countries of the WHO European Region. About 20% of children and adolescents are overweight, and a third of these are obese.

FIGURE 5.1 – Incidence of Pre-Obese and Obese Boys and Girls Aged 11 Years in a Number of European Countries

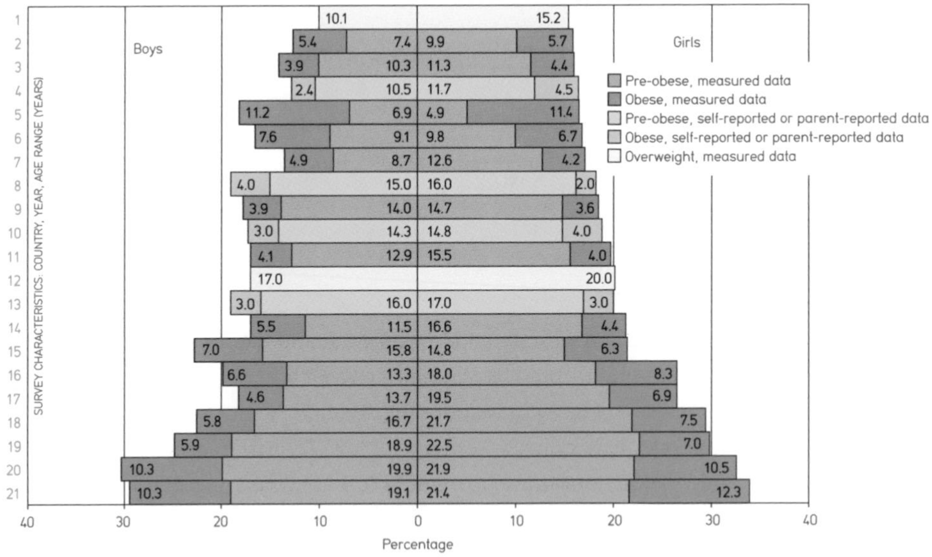

1 Germany: Aachen City, 2001-2002 · 2 Cyprus, 2004 · 3 Serbia and Montenegro: North Backa region, 1995-2002 · 4 Netherlands, 2005 · 5 Greece, 2003 · 6 Italy: Perugia, Terni and Rieti provinces, 1993-2001 · 7 Slovakia, 2001 · 8 Sweden, 2003 · 9 France, 2000 · 10 Norway, 2000 · 11 Switzerland, 2002-2003 · 12 Iceland, 2004 · 13 Sweden, 2003 · 14 Germany: Zerbst, Hettstedt and Bitterfeld counties, 1998-1999 · 15 Poland, 2000 · 16 Cyprus, 1999-2000 · 17 United Kingdom: three South Wales localities, 2001-2002 · 18 Ireland, 2001-2002 · 19 Italy: five villages in Milan province, 2000-2002 · 20 Spain, 1998-2000 · 21 Portugal, 2002-2003

Source: WHO, 2007[2]

- The prevalence of obesity is rising rapidly and is expected to include 150 million adults and 15 million children by 2010.
- The trend in obesity is especially alarming in children and adolescents. The annual rate of increase in the prevalence of childhood obesity has been growing steadily, and the current rate is 10 times that of the 1970s. See Figure 5.1.

It is recognised that obesity is a societal problem with both lifestyle factors, including diet, eating habits, levels of physical activity, and genetic factors being its cause. Not only is it a health risk in its own right, but it is also associated with an increase risk of diabetes, CVD and certain cancers. A cause for concern is that childhood obesity is a strong risk factor for adult obesity and obese children are likely to develop diabetes, heart disease and other chronic diseases earlier. Obesity and overweight create an enormous burden of disability and mortality and is estimated to be responsible for 10-15% life-years lost in the EU[2].

Monitoring Healthy Weight

A key measure when assessing weight management within a population is to establish the proportion with a healthy weight. The usual measure is body mass index (BMI). It's defined as body weight divided by the square of height and is reported in units of kg/m^2 (weight in kg)/(height in m)^2. A healthy weight is when the calculation results in a value of between 18.5 to 24.9 kg/m^2. The BMI for overweight is $\geq$ 25-30 kg/m^2 and obesity is defined as BMI of 30 or more. Waist to hip ratio provides an indication of central adiposity, considered to be a greater risk to health than those who carry their weight around the hips. A better and now frequently used measure of adiposity is waist circumference. Three categories each for men and women relate waist circumference to healthy weight, overweight and obesity, In the UK the higher two categories have been designated "action levels" 1 and 2 corresponding to slightly increased and substantially increased risk of chronic conditions such as CVD and diabetes.
Another measure of weight management is to measure weight gain over time. In general, as adults get older they tend to put on weight. Measuring the weight gain in kg over a relatively long period, say a year, or five years allows the identification of eating patterns more conducive to weight maintenance.

Maintaining Healthy Weight

WHO guidelines for promoting healthy behaviours to encourage, motivate and enable individuals to lose weight, recommend eating more fruit and vegetables, as well as nuts and whole-grains[3]. These recommendations are based on a review of the strength of evidence of factors that might promote or protect against weight gain and obesity. Factors were classified as being supported by convincing, probable, possible and insufficient evidence. The factors for which there was strongest evidence, identified as convincing, were regular physical activity and high intake of dietary fibre, which were protective whereas sedentary lifestyles and high dietary intake of energy-dense, micronutrient-poor foods increase the risk of weight gain. Those factors probably related to weight maintenance were home and school environments that support healthy food choices for children and breast feeding. While heavy marketing of energy-dense foods and fast-food outlets, high intake of sugars-sweetened soft drinks and fruit juices and, in developed countries, adverse socioeconomic conditions (especially for women) increased risk. A number of other factors were identified, but as yet there is either possible or insufficient evidence to draw conclusions. These factors include large portion size, a high proportion of food consumed outside the home and alcohol, which present a risk to weight maintenance. Low glycaemic index (GI) foods may be protective.

In the UK, the National Institute for Clinical Excellence (NICE) published guidance in December 2006 on the prevention, identification, assessment and management of overweight and obesity in adults and children. The first two NICE dietary guidelines for healthy weight maintenance make the following recommendations[4]:

- Base meals on starchy foods such as potatoes, bread, rice and pasta, choosing whole-grains wherever possible;
- Eat plenty of fibre-rich foods – such as oats, beans, peas, lentils, grains, seeds, fruit and vegetables, as well as whole-grain bread and brown rice and pasta.

Potential Benefits of Plant-Based Eating

Plant-based eating tends to be of lower energy density and promotes fibre intake (as discussed in Chapter 02) and as such follows the WHO dietary recommendations for weight management. Lower energy density is a result of both lower fat, particularly saturated fat intake, and higher fibre intake. The higher fibre content of plant-based eating patterns may be of direct benefit in weight management, as well as contributing to the lower energy density. Fibre, particularly soluble fibres, have been shown to contribute to feelings of fullness and improved satiety, which may be central to the role they play in weight management[5]. In addition most fibres are low glycaemic index which is important in glucose and particularly insulin management. Moderating insulin production or improving insulin sensitivity will tend to promote less fat storage and hence less obesity.

Scientific Evidence

In this area, observational studies can provide information about dietary patterns and weight maintenance over time. Or, by measuring BMI, can indicate the proportion of the population that are normal weight, overweight or obese. Short or medium term RCTs are often used to demonstrate the effectiveness of weight loss regimes. The better of these studies may be a year or two in duration. Shorter term RCTs may also be used to try an understand why particular eating patterns are effective in helping to maintain weight for example by measuring the satiation (feeling of fullness) or satiety characteristics of a food or eating pattern. Satiety is the decrease in motivation to eat after consuming food and varies in extent and duration. It may also result in a reduction in subsequent energy intake.

Observational Studies

Much of the observational study data comes from studies where subjects have been following vegetarian diets or a Mediterranean diet.

In a systematic review of cross sectional evidence it was consistently shown that an inverse relation exists between vegetarian diets and BMI in both adults and children[6]. In a meta analysis of 36 early studies conducted with adults, vegetarians had significantly lower weight (-7.7 kg for men and -3.3 kg for women; $P < 0.0001$ and $P = 0.007$, respectively) and 2-points lower BMI. There was no significant difference in height between vegetarians and non vegetarians[6].

Information from the Adventist studies provides an insight into weight management as people progress from, a vegan diet to mixed diet[6]. The data shown in

Figure 5.2, indicate there is a gradual increase in BMI as people progress to a mixed diet.

FIGURE 5.2 – BMI According to Vegetarian Status in the Adventist Health Study (BMI kg / m²)

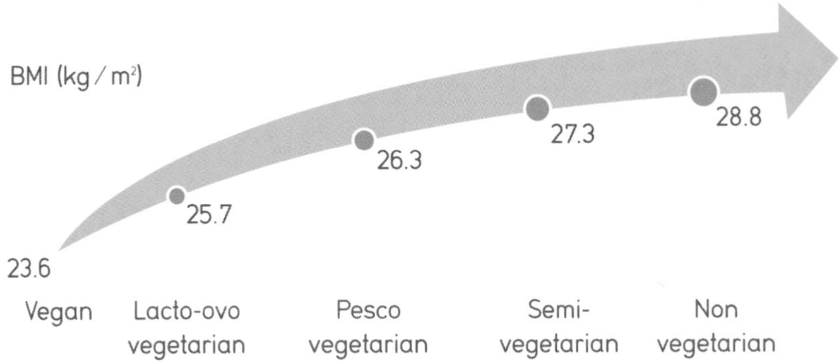

Source: Sabate and Wien[6]

Data from free-living European vegetarians is provided by the Oxford Vegetarian Study[7]. Dietary pattern data from 1914 men and 3378 women, aged 20 to 89 years, were compared to BMI. Lower BMI was observed in vegetarians compared with non vegetarians, by 1.1 kg/m^2 in men and 1.0kg/m^2 in women both highly statistically significant ($P < 0.001$). These findings are supported by the Oxford cohort of the European Prospective Investigation into Cancer and Nutrition (EPIC) study[8]. In 21,966 men and women, aged 20-69, participating in EPIC, the mean annual weight gain was 389g in men and 398g in women. When adjusted for a number of lifestyle factors, mean weight gain was less in vegans (284g in men and 303g in women, ($P < 0.05$)) and fish-eaters (338g, women only, $P < 0.001$) compared with meat-eaters. In Germany, an inverse relation between BMI and vegetarian status (strict vegetarian compared with occasional meat eater) was observed in a cohort of 20,000 vegetarians[9].

Further data is provided by an extensive study conducted in 10 European countries[10]. Here the adherence to the Mediterranean dietary pattern (MDP) was related to weight change and the incidence of overweight or obesity. This prospective cohort study [the European Prospective Investigation into Cancer and Nutrition-Physical Activity, Nutrition, Alcohol Consumption, Cessation of Smoking, Eating Out of Home, and Obesity (EPIC-PANACEA) project] was conducted in 373,803 individuals (103,455 men and 270,348 women), aged 25-70 years. Measurements were obtained at recruitment and after a median follow-up time of 5 years[10]. A Mediterranean Diet Score (range: 0-18) was developed to assess adherence the Mediterranean diet. The association between the Mediterranean Diet Score and weight change over 5 years was modeled. Individuals with a high adherence to the Mediterranean Diet (11-18 points) showed a modest 5-year weight change of -0.16 kg and were 10% less likely to become overweight or develop obesity than were individuals with a low score (0-6 points).

A plant-based eating regime was assessed by comparing dietary patterns using data from the USA, specifically from the Nurse's Health Study[11]. Consumption of a diet that was high in fruit and vegetables, whole-grains, fish and poultry, and low-fat dairy products, a so-called "prudent diet", was compared to a typical Western-style diet. In this study 51,670 women aged 26 to 46 years were followed from 1991 to 1999. Dietary intake and body weight were obtained in 1991, 1995, and 1999. Women who increased their Western pattern score had greater weight gain (4.55 kg for 1991 to 1995 and 2.86 kg for 1995 to 1999) than women who decreased their Western pattern score (2.70 kg and 1.37 kg for the two time periods), ($P < 0.001$). While in women who increased their prudent pattern score, weight gain was less (1.93 kg, and 0.66 kg respectively for the two time periods) ($P < 0.001$). The largest weight gain between 1991 and 1995 and between 1995 and 1999 was observed among women who decreased their prudent pattern score while increasing their Western pattern score (6.80 and 4.99 kg respectively) and it was smallest for the opposite change in patterns (0.87 and -0.64 kg) ($P < 0.001$).

Less is known about vegetarian diets in children, but early studies have shown that vegetarian children tend to be leaner than non vegetarian children. Concern about growth rate and height attainment has been shown in more recent times not to be substantiated, although maturity may be reached later. The association of protein intake from either plant or animal sources in early and mid-childhood was associated with the ages at take-off of the pubertal growth spurt (ATO), peak height velocity, menarche in girls and voice break in boys using data from the Dortmund Nutritional and Anthropometric Longitudinally Designed Study[12]. A higher total and animal protein intake at age 5-6 years was related to an earlier ATO. In those in the highest third of animal protein intake at age 5-6 years, ATO occurred 0.6 years earlier than those in the lowest (P for trend = 0.003). Similar findings were seen for peak height velocity (P for trend = 0.001) and the timing of menarche/voice break (P for trend = 0.02). Conversely, a higher vegetable protein intake at ages 3-4 and 5-6 years was related to later ATO, peak height velocity and menarche/voice break (P-trend =

0.02-0.04). These results suggest that animal and vegetable protein intake in mid-childhood might be differentially related to pubertal timing.

A recent review on the role of plant foods and plant-based diets in protecting against childhood obesity showed no relation with fruit and vegetables; insufficient evidence with beans, legumes, and soy; and slight protection with grains and breakfast cereals, fibre, and plant-based dietary patterns[13]. The studies reviewed were largely cross sectional and most had some methodological limitations leading the authors to call for further well-conducted research. Nevertheless they concluded that the advice to consume a plant-based, low-energy-dense diet was sound.

Overall the evidence from observational studies indicates that, those who follow plant-based eating, such as vegetarians or Mediterranean diet, tend to have a lower BMI and gain less weight over time.

Clinical Studies

The objective of short term clinical studies is often to establish the effectiveness of various weight-loss regimes rather than to look at weight management over time. One of the few studies specifically conducted with plant-based diets evaluated the weight loss in volunteers following a plant-based so-called, "Eco-Atkins" diet and compared this to a more conventional low-carbohydrate, high-animal protein weight-reducing diet[14]. In this 4 week-parallel design study, 47 overweight hyperlipidemic men and women consumed isocaloric diets that comprised either:

- a low-carbohydrate (26%), high-vegetable protein (31% from gluten, soy, nuts, fruit, vegetables, and cereals), and vegetable oil (43%) plant-based diet

or

- a high-carbohydrate lacto-ovo vegetarian diet (58% carbohydrate, 16% protein, and 25% fat).

At the end of the 4-week period weight loss was similar at 4kg, equivalent to around 4.8% of body weight (bwt), as was the percentage of weight lost as body fat. A major difference between treatments was the blood lipid profile which was significantly improved with the Eco-Atkins diet with TC, LDL-C and TAG all significantly reduced ($P < 0.002$). Both systolic blood pressure (–1.9%, $P = 0.05$)

and diastolic blood pressure (−2.4% P = 0.02), were also lower resulting in an overall lower risk of heart disease.

High protein, low carbohydrate diets have been associated with improved weight loss in studies of 3-6 months duration[15], but few studies have looked at the importance of the source of protein. Around 10 RCTs were identified that compared different protein sources, usually animal protein compared to soya protein. There are a number of imperfections in these studies, but when the findings from eight studies conducted with soya protein were pooled, the weight loss in 4-week periods was 2.7kg with soya protein and 2.4kg with the control protein[16]. See Figure 5.3.

FIGURE 5.3 – Four-Week Weight Loss in RCT with Soya and Control Treatments

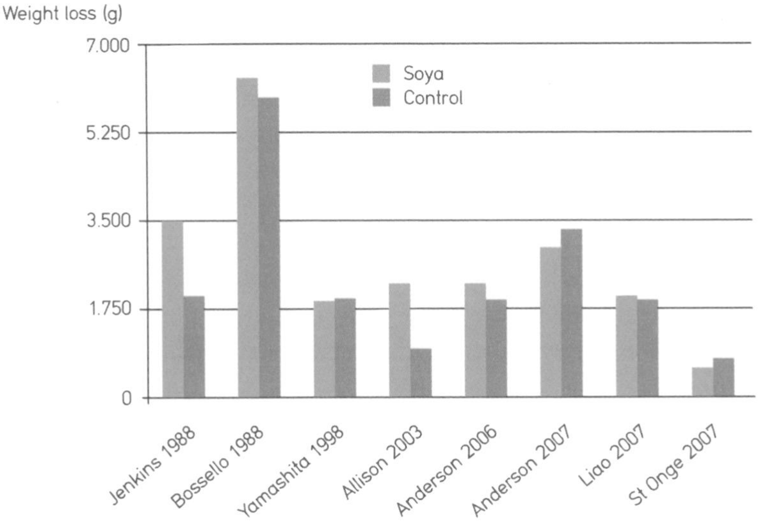

Source: Harland 2008[16]

In a 9-week study conducted in 54 postmenopausal women aged 58 years and with an average BMI of 29.6, protein source was compared in three energy-reduced diets[17]. The basal lacto-ovo vegetarian energy-reduced diet provided 1000 kcal/d and was supplemented by 250kcal/d of beef, chicken or carbohydrate/fat foods (CARB lacto-ovo). It is unfortunate that protein intakes differed between the groups and were 25%e in the beef and chicken groups and 17%e in the lacto-ovo vegetarian group. The weight loss over the 9-week period was greatest in the chicken group at -7.9kg (10.4% bwt), which was significantly more than in the CARB lacto-ovo (-5.9kg) (7.7% bwt) with the beef group being similar (8.1% bwt). In a second trial from this group, a diet where protein provided 18%e from lacto-ovo vegetarian sources was compared to a diet of 30%e from protein, where 40% of this protein was derived from lean pork. Weight loss in this study was similar at 11.2% and 10.1% of bwt in lacto-ovo vegetarian and pork groups respectively[17]. In a further study, a standard weight loss regime was compared to a lacto-ovo vegetarian regime. Approximately half of the participants expressed a preference for the regime that they wished to follow. The remaining subjects were randomly assigned to either the standard or the lacto-ovo vegetarian diet. Weight loss in these 176 postmenopausal women was monitored over 18 months. There was no significant difference between the two dietary treatments although those randomly assigned to treatments tended to lose more weight (7.9% and 8.1% bwt for standard and lacto-ovo vegetarian respectively) compared to those who choose the regime they followed (3.9% and 5.3% bwt for standard and lacto-ovo vegetarian respectively)[18]. Changes in blood lipid profile were marginally improved in the lacto-ovo vegetarian groups (P = 0.06).

It appears that weight-reducing diets based on plant-based foods are as effective as standard weight loss diets that include meat, although there is some evidence that blood lipid profile may be improved, thereby reducing heart disease risk.

The effects of three energy matched diets on 24-h energy expenditure have been compared. The diets were based on meat protein (pork), a vegetable protein (soya), and carbohydrate[19]. Substitution of carbohydrate (carb) with 17-18%e as either pork-meat or soya protein produced a 3% higher 24-h energy expenditure. Diet induced thermogenesis (heat production) and basic metabolic rate also tended to be higher in the protein diets indicating that these factors may contribute to weight loss. See Table 5.1.

TABLE 5.1 – The Effect of Protein Source Compared to Carbohydrate on 24-hour Energy Expenditure

	Pork	Soya	Carb	Baseline
Diet-induced thermogenesis kJ/min	9.08^{a}	8.77^{a}	8.61^{b}	8.75^{ab}
Basal metabolic rate kJ/min	6.90^{a}	6.73^{ab}	6.60^{b}	6.57^{b}
24-h Energy expenditure (MJ/d)	13.11^{a}	12.86^{b}	12.62^{c}	12.52^{bc}

Values with different superscript letters are significantly different ($P < 0.05$)
Source: Mikkelsen, 2000[19]

Another important factor for weight maintenance is the effectiveness of the dietary pattern on appetite regulation and satiety. It is well established that proteins, fats and carbohydrates generate different sets of physiological responses that produce different effects on the intensity and duration of satiety[20]. Generally it is believed that protein is more satiating, it leads to higher rate of thermogenesis and helps to maintain fat-free body weight[21]. The overall nutrient composition of food and energy density also influence appetite regulation. Particular sensory and nutrient combinations (for example, saturated fat and salt in meat pies and pastries; saturated fat and sugar in cakes and confectionary) in foods can lead to passive overconsumption, while overriding the physiological satiety signals can lead to a positive energy balance and weight gain. The relative importance of these factors has yet to be established in plant-based eating.

Overall it is believed that there may be three reasons that explain the differences in BMI observed between vegetarians and non vegetarians. Firstly, the avoidance of meat that contains saturated fatty acids and is greater in energy density may be beneficial in weight management. Meat avoidance may be too simplistic and it may be the requirement for relatively low ratios of saturated to unsaturated fats that is important. This is because saturated fat impairs insulin sensitivity and in response insulin secretion is stimulated, which in turn promotes lipid uptake into fatty tissues and increases body fat[22]. It may also be the ratio of essential to non-essential amino acids that are beneficial and these happen to be found in plant-based diets[22]. The higher fibre content of plant-based eating patterns also contributes to their lower energy density, whether the benefit in weight management is from the fibre itself or an indirect effect due to energy density is an area that requires further research[23]. Certain soluble fibres have been shown to contribute to feelings of fullness and improved satiety[5].

Secondly plant-based eating tends to be associated with other beneficial lifestyle factors, including less smoking, greater physical activity, and higher education level that may influence body weight. It may well be the combination of all of these factors that are important rather than a single factor[24].

Finally, the variety of plant foods that evolves into a plant-based eating pattern may have a significant influence preventing overweight or obesity and on weight maintenance through the action of specific factors present in plant foods that possibly promote appetite regulation and satiety.

Plant-based eating is associated with lower body weight and less weight gain over time.

Plant-based foods and eating patterns are typically low in saturated fat, and high in unsaturated fats and fibre. This may be important in maintaining body weight.

Specific components found intrinsically in plant foods may work together to help with appetite regulation and promoting satiety.

Eating more fruit, vegetables, legumes, whole-grains, nuts and seeds and reducing the amount of energy-rich foods, is a simple and easy way to help manage weight.

Literature chapter 05

1. Commision of the European Communities, *White Paper: A Strategy for Europe on Nutrition, Overweight and Obesity related health issues.* COM(2007) 279 final, 2007.
2. WHO, *The challenge of obesity in the WHO European Region and the strategies for response* ed. F. Branca, H. Nikogosian, and T. Lobstein. 2007, Copenhagen, Denmark: WHO Europe.
3. WHO. *5.2 Recommendations for preventing excess weight gain and obesity, p61-71.* 2003.
4. NICE. *Obesity: guidance on the prevention, identification and management of obesity and overweight in adults and children.* NICE National Institute for Health and Clinical Excellence, clinical publication 43. 2006.
5. Howarth, N.C., E. Saltzman, and S.B. Roberts, *Dietary fiber and weight regulation.* Nutr Rev, 2001. **59**(5): p. 129-39.
6. Sabate, J. and M. Wien, *Vegetarian diets and childhood obesity prevention.* Am J Clin Nutr, 2010. **91**(5): p. 1525S-1529S.
7. Appleby, P.N., et al., *Low body mass index in non-meat eaters: the possible roles of animal fat, dietary fibre and alcohol.* Int J Obes Relat Metab Disord, 1998. **22**(5): p. 454-60.
8. Rosell, M., et al., *Weight gain over 5 years in 21,966 meat-eating, fish-eating, vegetarian, and vegan men and women in EPIC-Oxford.* Int J Obes (Lond), 2006. **30**(9): p. 1389-96.
9. Chang-Claude, J. and R. Frentzel-Beyme, *Dietary and lifestyle determinants of mortality among German vegetarians.* Int J Epidemiol, 1993. **22**(2): p. 228-36.
10. Romaguera, D., et al., *Mediterranean dietary patterns and prospective weight change in participants of the EPIC-PANACEA project.* Am J Clin Nutr, 2010. **92**(4): p. 912-21.
11. Schulze, M.B., et al., *Dietary patterns and changes in body weight in women.* Obesity (Silver Spring), 2006. **14**(8): p. 1444-53.
12. Gunther, A.L., et al., *Dietary protein intake throughout childhood is associated with the timing of puberty.* J Nutr, 2010. **140**(3): p. 565-71.
13. Newby, P.K., *Plant foods and plant-based diets: protective against childhood obesity?* Am J Clin Nutr, 2009. **89**(5): p. 1572S-1587S.
14. Jenkins, D.J., et al., *The effect of a plant-based low-carbohydrate ("Eco-Atkins") diet on body weight and blood lipid concentrations in hyperlipidemic subjects.* Arch Intern Med, 2009. **169**(11): p. 1046-54.
15. Foster, G.D., et al., *A randomized trial of a low-carbohydrate diet for obesity.* N Engl J Med, 2003. **348**(21): p. 2082-90.
16. Harland, J.I., *Soy protein in the diets of overweight & obese: a systematic review of the evidence*, in *Soy and Health* 2008: Bruges, Belgium.
17. Campbell, W.W. and M. Tang, *Protein intake, weight loss, and bone mineral density in postmenopausal women.* J Gerontol A Biol Sci Med Sci, 2010. **65**(10): p. 1115-22.
18. Burke, L.E., et al., *Effects of a vegetarian diet and treatment preference on biochemical and dietary variables in overweight and obese adults: a randomized clinical trial.* Am J Clin Nutr, 2007. **86**(3): p. 588-96.
19. Mikkelsen, P.B., S. Toubro, and A. Astrup, *Effect of fat-reduced diets on 24-h energy expenditure: comparisons between animal protein, vegetable protein, and carbohydrate.* Am J Clin Nutr, 2000. **72**(5): p. 1135-41.
20. Blundell, J.E. and N.A. King, *Overconsumption as a cause of weight gain: behavioural-physiological interactions in the control of food intake (appetite).* Ciba Found Symp, 1996. **201**: p. 138-54; discussion 154-8, 188-93.
21. Paddon-Jones, D., et al., *Protein, weight management, and satiety.* Am J Clin Nutr, 2008. **87**(5): p. 1558S-1561S.
22. McCarty, M.F., *Dietary saturate/unsaturate ratio as a determinant of adiposity.* Med Hypotheses, 2010. **75**(1): p. 14-6.
23. Howarth, N.C., et al., *Eating patterns and dietary composition in relation to BMI in younger and older adults.* Int J Obes (Lond), 2006.
24. Harland, J.I. and L.E. Garton, *Whole-grain intake as a marker of healthy body weight and adiposity.* Public Health Nutr, 2007: p. 1-10.

06

Chapter 06

Plant-Based Eating and Managing Blood Glucose

Summary

- Maintaining blood glucose (sugar) at healthy levels is important for good health.
- In the WHO European region in 2000, it was estimated that 33 million people had diabetes and this is thought to increase to 48 million by 2030.
- To help prevent Type 2 diabetes and its complications, it's recommended that people maintain a healthy body weight, be physically active, avoid smoking and eat a healthy diet rich in fruit and vegetables, as well as nuts and whole-grains.
- Evidence from observational studies indicates those who follow plant-based eating, such as vegetarians or vegans, tend to develop less diabetes over time and have better blood glucose control.
- Interventions that increase the intake of fibre-rich plant foods demonstrate improved blood glucose control and insulin sensitivity, better weight management, and reductions in markers of inflammation and heart disease.
- Plant-based eating is associated with less energy dense diets that are lower in saturated fat and rich in fibre, as well as lifestyle factors that are associated with better blood glucose management.

Challenge of Diabetes in Europe

The prime indication of poor blood glucose management is the development of diabetes. The World Health Organisation (WHO) estimates that more than 220 million people worldwide have diabetes. In the WHO European region in 2000, it was estimated that 33 million people had diabetes and this is thought to increase to 48 million by 2030. The WHO projects diabetes deaths will double between 2005 and 2030 and is extremely concerned by the rate of increase[1].

TABLE 6.1: Reported Level of Diabetes in Certain European Countries and Projected Levels in 2030

European Country	Prevalence 2000	Predicted prevalence in 2030
Belgium	317,000	461,000
France	1,710,000	2,645,000
Germany	2,627,000	3,771,000
Italy	4,252,000	5,374,000
The Netherlands	426,000	720,000
Spain	2,717,000	3,752,000
Turkey	2,920,000	6,422,000
UK	1,765,000	2,668,000

Source: WHO

The challenge of diabetes is not only related to the condition itself, but associated with diabetes are a number of complications that can result in damage to the heart, blood vessels, eyes, kidneys, and nerves[1]. Specifically diabetes...

- Increases the risk of heart disease and stroke, with half of the people with diabetes dying of CVD (primarily heart disease and stroke).
- Combined with reduced blood flow, increases the chance of foot ulcers and eventual limb amputation.
- Is an important cause of blindness, and occurs as a result of long-term accumulated damage to the small blood vessels in the retina in the eye.
- Is among the leading causes of kidney failure.
- Can result in damage to the nerves which affects up to half the people with diabetes.
- Increases the overall risk of dying which is at least double the risk of those without diabetes.

Consequently not only is it important to maintain healthy blood glucose levels to reduce the risk of developing diabetes but also to help avoid the risk of developing ill health and a wide range of chronic diseases.

Identifying Diabetes

Diabetes is a chronic disease that occurs either when the pancreas does not produce enough insulin, or when the body cannot effectively use the insulin it produces. Insulin is a hormone that regulates blood sugar. Hyperglycaemia, or raised blood glucose, is a common effect of uncontrolled diabetes and over time leads to serious damage to many of the body's systems, especially the nerves and blood vessels.

There are a number of types of diabetes which include:

Type 1 diabetes sometimes known as insulin-dependent, juvenile or childhood-onset diabetes. It occurs as a result of not enough insulin being produced and requires daily administration of insulin. The cause of Type 1 diabetes is not known and based on our current knowledge it's not preventable.

Type 2 diabetes sometimes known as non-insulin-dependent or adult-onset diabetes. It results when the body can still make some insulin, but not enough, or when the insulin that is produced does not work effectively (insulin resistance). Type 2 diabetes comprises 90% of people with diabetes around the world, and is largely the result of excess body weight and physical inactivity.

Until recently, this type of diabetes was seen only in adults but it is now also occurring in children.

Gestational diabetes is elevated blood glucose levels that arises during pregnancy.

Prediabetes, also known as impaired glucose tolerance (IGT) or impaired fasting glycaemia (IFG), occurs when glucose levels are higher than normal but not high enough to be diagnosed as diabetes. People with IGT or IFG are at high risk of progressing to Type 2 diabetes, although this is not inevitable.

Avoiding the development of Type 2 diabetes will be the focus of this chapter and where the term diabetes is used, it refers to Type 2 diabetes. The criteria used to define diabetes, impaired glucose tolerance and the metabolic syndrome are given in Table 6.2.

TABLE 6.2 - 2006 WHO Diabetes Criteria

Condition	2 hour glucose* mmol/L	Fasting glucose mmol/L
Normal	<7.8	<6.1
Impaired fasting glycaemia	<7.8	≥ 6.1 & <7.0
Impaired glucose tolerance	≥7.8	<7.0
Diabetes mellitus	≥11.1	≥7.0

* Two hours after a 75g oral glucose load in a glucose tolerance test.

Maintaining Healthy Glucose Levels

Lifestyle measures have been shown to be effective in preventing or delaying the onset of Type 2 diabetes. To help prevent Type 2 diabetes and its complications, it's recommended that people should:

- achieve and maintain a healthy body weight;
- be physically active – at least 30 minutes of regular, moderate-intensity activity on most days, a greater level of activity is required for weight control;
- eat a healthy diet;
- avoid tobacco use – smoking increases the risk of cardiovascular diseases.

The WHO *Global strategy on diet, physical activity and health* complements WHO's diabetes work by focusing on population-wide approaches to promote healthy diet and regular physical activity, thereby reducing the growing global problem of overweight and obesity[2].

Its dietary recommendations include:

- limit energy intake from total fats and shift fat consumption away from saturated fats to unsaturated fats and towards the elimination of trans fatty acids;
- increase consumption of fruits and vegetables, and legumes, whole-grains and nuts;

- limit the intake of free sugars;
- limit salt (sodium) consumption from all sources and ensure that salt is iodized.

Potential Benefits of Plant-based Eating

Maintaining glucose levels within the healthy range will help avoid the development of diabetes. It maybe the higher fibre content of plant-based eating patterns that are of direct benefit in glucose management[3]. Fibre, particularly soluble fibres, may result in more desirable blood glucose levels after a meal (post prandial glucose concentrations (glucose tolerance curve)) or insulin response[4-5]. In addition, most fibres have a low glycaemic index (GI). This index is a ranking of foods based on their overall effect on blood glucose levels. Low GI carbohydrates produce only small fluctuations in blood glucose and insulin levels and as such are beneficial in helping to manage diabetes and also reducing the risk of heart disease[6]. The glycemic load (GL) is a ranking system for carbohydrate content in food portions based on their GI and the portion size. GL combines both the quality and quantity of carbohydrate in one 'number'. It is used to predict blood glucose values of different types and amounts of food. The basic formula is:
GL = (GI x the amount of available carbohydrate) divided by 100.

Fibres tend to have both a low GI and a low GL, and as such will tend to moderate insulin production thereby improving insulin sensitivity and tending to promote less fat storage and reducing the risk of both diabetes and obesity.

Conditions which predispose to developing diabetes, include overweight (and obesity), reduced insulin sensitivity, and inflammation. Consequently any aspect of plant-based eating that can help to improve these will help to avoid progressing to diabetes. Plant-based eating patterns tend to be lower in energy density and promote fibre intake as discussed in Chapter 02 and as such follows the WHO dietary recommendations. Lower energy density is a result of both lower fat, particularly SFA intake, and higher fibre intake and is beneficial in weight management, see Chapter 05.

It's believed that eating large amounts of calorie-dense foods causes abnormal surges in blood glucose and triglyceride (TAG) levels[7]. After a meal high levels of certain fats in the blood including TAG, chylomicrons and remnant lipoproteins cause oxidative stress and inflammation. This can also have a negative impact on blood glucose levels after a meal[7]. Consequently eating patterns that blunt the post meal glucose and TAG response are beneficial in maintaining healthy glucose tolerance[8].

Scientific Evidence

Observational studies can provide information about dietary patterns and development of diabetes over time. Or, by measuring insulin sensitivity, glucose tolerance or some other factor, dietary patterns can indicate the risk of developing diabetes. Clinical studies (RCTs) are often used to demonstrate the effectiveness of specific dietary components on glucose levels or insulin sensitivity.

Observational Studies

There are few observational studies that have specifically looked at the relationship between plant-based eating and diabetes. In the main, data comes from studies where subjects have been following vegetarian or vegan diets, or dietary intake is reviewed relative to the intake of fibre, whole-grain cereals or meat.

The Dutch European Prospective Investigation into Cancer and Nutrition (EPIC) cohort comprises of 38,094 subjects, aged 21-70 y at baseline and followed for 10 years. It has been used to demonstrate that diabetes risk increases with higher total protein intake (hazard ratio (HR) 2.15 for the highest vs. lowest quartile) and animal protein intake (HR, 2.18), whereas vegetable protein was not related to diabetes[9]. The authors calculated that consuming 5%e from total or animal protein at the expense of 5%e from carbohydrates or fat increased diabetes risk. In the same cohort, it was established that dietary fibre intake was associated with an 8% reduced diabetes risk (HR, 0.92; $P < 0.05$), but increasing glycaemic load and glycaemic index of the diet resulted in a greater risk of diabetes, (HR, 1.32; $P < 0.001$ and 1.08; $P = 0.05$ respectively)[10].

Other studies have identified that higher red meat consumption is associated with an increased risk of developing diabetes. For example in middle-aged women in The Women's Health Study[11]; in men in The Health Professionals Follow-Up Study[12]; and in women of child-bearing age a greater risk of developing gestational diabetes was identified in The Nurses' Health Study II[13]. Using data from the Seventh-day Adventist Study II, which contains data from 22,434 men and 38,469 women, approximately half of whom are omnivores and half vegetarians, it has been shown that for a range of diets, as the consumption of meat and animal products increase, there is an increasing prevalence of diabetes[14], see Figure 6.1.

In a recent systematic review of 12 cohort studies, including those already detailed, it has been estimated that the relative risk of developing diabetes was 17% higher when comparing high or low intake of red meat. Or expressed another way, for each 120g increase in red meat intake (equivalent to a small piece of steak), the risk of developing diabetes was 20% higher[15]. A similar comparison that evaluated the risk of developing diabetes compared to total meat intake, indicated a 21% greater risk at higher intakes[15].

FIGURE 6.1 - The Effect of Eating Pattern on Type 2 Diabetes Prevalence in The Adventist Health Study II.

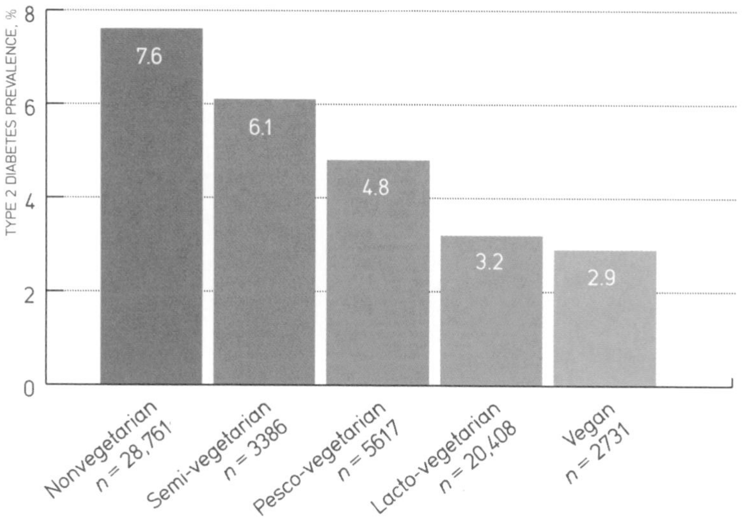

Source: Trapp and Barnard 2010[15]

Eating patterns rich in whole-grain foods have also been shown to be associated with a lower risk of developing diabetes. Using data from three prospective studies, including 160,000 men and women, it was identified that the risk of developing Type 2 diabetes was 21-27% lower for those in the highest quintile of whole-grain intake (typically those consuming two or more servings of whole-grain foods compared to those consuming little or none), and 30-36% lower in the highest quintile of cereal-fibre intake, each compared with the lowest quintile[17].

The Isfahan Diabetes Prevention Study is a cross-sectional study conducted in 425 Iranian subjects aged 35 to 55 years[18]. It evaluated the effect of dietary patterns on blood pressure, waist circumference, glucose, TAG, and HDL-C and metabolic syndrome as defined by the Adult Treatment Panel III guidelines. Five major dietary patterns were found:

- a western pattern (high in sweets, butter, soda, mayonnaise, sugar, cookies, lamb, hydrogenated fat, and eggs),
- a prudent pattern (high in fish, peas, honey, nuts, juice, dry fruits, vegetable oil, liver and organic meat, and coconuts and low in hydrogenated fat and non-leafy vegetables),
- a vegetarian pattern (high in potatoes, legumes, fruits rich in vitamin C, rice, green leafy vegetables, and fruits rich in vitamin A),
- a high-fat dairy pattern (high in high-fat yoghurt and high-fat milk and low in low-fat yoghurt, peas, and bread), and
- a chicken and plant pattern (high in chicken, fruits rich in vitamin A, green leafy vegetables, and mayonnaise and low in beef, liver, and organic meat).

Positive significant associations were observed between the western dietary pattern and blood TAG, BP and the metabolic syndrome. While the vegetarian dietary pattern was inversely associated with a risk of an abnormal fasting blood glucose level (odds ratio, 2.26).

Associations between dietary fibre and magnesium intake and risk of Type 2 diabetes were examined by means of meta analysis[3]. Nine cohort studies that measured fibre intake were assessed and an overall relative risk calculated. Meta-analyses showed a 33% reduced risk of diabetes with higher cereal fibre intake. Fruit and vegetable fibre intakes were not significantly associated with diabetes risk.

Clinical Studies

The number of RCTs that examine the relationship between plant-based eating and risk of diabetes is limited. In a recent systematic review 13 RCTs were identified but, in fact, the majority reported a relationship between either insoluble or soluble fibre and some measure of diabetes risk[5]. Only four studies, all of which were conducted in diabetics, specifically studied plant-based diets. Of these, three RCTs related to vegan diets, rather than the broader definition of plant-based eating adopted in Introduction.

In the first of these three studies a low fat plant-based diet (<10%e fat and 26g fibre) was compared to a control diet that met the American Diabetic Association 2003 guidelines (15-20%e protein, <7%e SFA, 60-70%e carbohydrate and 20g fibre) as part of a pilot study with 11 overweight, Type 2 diabetic men and women[19]. The diets were not designed to be isocaloric and, as a result, weight loss was markedly different between the two groups with the control group losing 3.8 kg and the experimental group 7.2 kg ($P < 0.005$). The vegan diet also resulted in a 28% mean reduction in fasting serum glucose from 10.7 to 7.75 mmol/L, which was significantly greater than the 12% decrease, from 9.86 to 8.64 mmol/L, in the control group ($P < 0.05$). No other measures of glycaemic control were significantly altered, although blood lipid profile improved.

In a second study with 99 overweight diabetics, the macronutrient targets of the control and experimental diets were as previously described, except the vegan and control diets resulted in fibre intakes of 36.3g and 19g respectively[20]. Volunteers were evaluated at baseline and after 22 weeks. At the end of study, 43% of subjects (21 of 49) in the vegan group and 26% (13 of 50) of the control group reduced their diabetes medications. Glycated haemoglobin (HbA(1c)) decreased non significantly by 0.96 and 0.56 percentage points in the vegan and control groups respectively ($P=0.089$). When those diabetics who had changed medications were excluded, HbA(1c) fell 1.23 points in the vegan group compared with 0.38 points in the control group ($P = 0.01$). Urine albumin was also significantly reduced in the vegan group. As in the previous study, body weight loss was greater in the vegan group than in the control group (6.5 kg compared to 3.1 kg), ($P < 0.001$). In a further report of this study, after volunteers had been on their respective diets for 74 weeks[21], changes in HbA(1c) from baseline to 74 weeks (or last available value), or last value before any medication adjustment, were -0.40 and 0.01 for vegan and control groups, respectively ($P=0.03$). Weight loss was sustained over the 74 week period, but was not significantly different between groups (-4.4 kg in the vegan group and -3.0 kg in the control group). Significant reductions in both Total -C and LDL-C were also reported in the vegan group. After controlling for medication changes the authors concluded that, a low-fat vegan diet appeared to improve glycaemia and plasma lipids more than the conventional diabetes dietary recommendations.

In the final RCT identified, a plant-based, high carbohydrate/high fibre diet (52% carbohydrate and 28g fibre) was compared to a low carbohydrate/high MUFA diet (45% carbohydrate, 23% MUFA and 8g fibre)[22]. The 4-week study was crossover in design and was conducted in 18 marginally overweight men and women with diabetes. In the plant-based period, there were significant decreases in after meal plasma glucose levels and insulin responses. The plant-based diet also significantly improved markers of inflammation and coronary health, as well as improved glycaemic control, suggesting that plant-based eating may be beneficial for diabetics.

Dietary intake, including protein amount and type, seems to affect the progression of renal disease an important consideration for those with diabetes. A pilot study tested the hypothesis that substituting a vegetable protein for animal protein in the diets of diabetics would help correct kidney function in terms of glomerular hyperfiltration. In this small study with 12 young adults (aged 29.9) with Type 1 diabetes mellitus, glomerular filtration rate was shown to be improved after eight weeks, both compared to baseline and compared to a control based on animal protein demonstrating an overall improved clinical profile in these diabetics[23].

A number of RCTs have assessed the effect of fibre or addition of whole-grain on a number of measures of glycaemic control and have reported improvements[5]. For example, when overweight women without diabetes consumed additional insoluble fibre (total intake 31.2g/day), insulin sensitivity improved by 8% and there was a 12% increase in insulin action compared to the control[24]. The addition of soluble fibre in the form of beta glucan led to improved post-meal glucose tolerance and resulted in a lower insulin response (33% less) when introduced into the diet of overweight non-diabetic women[25]. Two studies assessed the addition of whole-grain cereals on insulin resistance score[26-27]. In men with coronary artery disease with, or without diabetes, and in obese men and women the score was significantly improved indicating that the insulin was performing at a more optimal efficiency level.

Overview and Conclusions

Based on what is known of the components of plant-based diets and the findings from clinical studies in the literature, it appears there is sufficient evidence to indicate that those following plant-based eating have improved glycaemia, i.e. better management of blood glucose.

In addition, observational studies indicate diabetes prevalence is lower in those following a vegan or vegetarian diet. Whereas consuming more meat and animal products tend to result in a higher incidence of diabetes. As meat can be a significant source of SFA in the diet, whether it is a property of meat per se, or other nutrients associated with a meat-rich diet, is not absolutely clear. For example, it has been suggested that substituting vegetable proteins for animal protein may also decrease the long term risk of developing kidney disease in Type 2 diabetes[28].

Certainly the information presented in Chapter 05, indicates that plant-based eating is associated with better weight management, and as obesity is one of the key risk factors in the development of diabetes, then it may be this aspect that is of importance.

Data from clinical studies with plant foods have indicated improvements in markers of inflammation and CVD, as well as glycaemic control and insulin sensitivity. It may well be the combination of all these aspects of plant-based eating patterns that are of value to those wishing to maintain healthy glucose levels and avoid the progression to diabetes.

Plant-based eating is associated with better blood glucose control.

Incidence of diabetes is increasing and is associated with an increased risk of obesity, heart conditions and other chronic diseases.

Plant-based foods and eating patterns are typically low in saturated fat, and rich in fibre. Fibre is important as it helps glycaemic control, may improve satiety and is useful in maintaining body weight.

Eating more fruit, vegetables, legumes, whole-grains, nuts and seeds and reducing the amount of energy-rich foods, is a simple and easy way to improve blood glucose control and help manage some of the risks associated with diabetes, such as obesity and heart disease.

Literature chapter 06

1. World Heath Organisation, Diabetes Fact sheet N°312. 2011, http://www.who.int/mediacentre/factsheets/fs312/en/index.html.
2. World Health Organization, Global Strategy on Diet, Physical Activity and Health. 2004, http://www.who.int/dietphysicalactivity/strategy/eb11344/en/index.html.
3. Schulze, M.B., et al., Fiber and magnesium intake and incidence of type 2 diabetes: a prospective study and meta-analysis. Arch Intern Med, 2007. **167**(9): p. 956-65.
4. Anderson, J.W., et al., Health benefits of dietary fiber. Nutr Rev, 2009. **67**(4): p. 188-205.
5. Wolfram, T. and F. Ismail-Beigi, Efficacy of diets containing high amounts of fiber in the management of type 2 diabetes. Endocr Pract, 2010: p. 1-27.
6. Anderson, J.W., et al., Carbohydrate and fiber recommendations for individuals with diabetes: a quantitative assessment and meta-analysis of the evidence. J Am Coll Nutr, 2004. **23**(1): p. 5-17.
7. O'Keefe, J.H., N.M. Gheewala, and J.O. O'Keefe, Dietary strategies for improving post-prandial glucose, lipids, inflammation, and cardiovascular health. J Am Coll Cardiol, 2008. **51**(3): p. 249-55.
8. Lichtenstein, A.H., et al., Diet and lifestyle recommendations revision 2006: a scientific statement from the American Heart Association Nutrition Committee. Circulation, 2006. **114**(1): p. 82-96.
9. Sluijs, I., et al., Dietary intake of total, animal, and vegetable protein and risk of type 2 diabetes in the European Prospective Investigation into Cancer and Nutrition (EPIC)-NL study. Diabetes Care, 2010. **33**(1): p. 43-8.
10. Sluijs, I., et al., Carbohydrate quantity and quality and risk of type 2 diabetes in the European Prospective Investigation into Cancer and Nutrition-Netherlands (EPIC-NL) study. Am J Clin Nutr, 2010. **92**(4): p. 905-11.
11. Song, Y., et al., A prospective study of red meat consumption and type 2 diabetes in middle-aged and elderly women: the women's health study. Diabetes Care, 2004. **27**(9): p. 2108-15.
12. van Dam, R.M., et al., Dietary patterns and risk for type 2 diabetes mellitus in U.S. men. Ann Intern Med, 2002. **136**(3): p. 201-9.
13. Zhang, C., et al., A prospective study of dietary patterns, meat intake and the risk of gestational diabetes mellitus. Diabetologia, 2006. **49**(11): p. 2604-13.
14. Tonstad, S., et al., Type of vegetarian diet, body weight, and prevalence of type 2 diabetes. Diabetes Care, 2009. **32**(5): p. 791-6.
15. Aune, D., G. Ursin, and M.B. Veierod, Meat consumption and the risk of type 2 diabetes: a systematic review and meta-analysis of cohort studies. Diabetologia, 2009. **52**(11): p. 2277-87.
16. Trapp, C.B. and N.D. Barnard, Usefulness of vegetarian and vegan diets for treating type 2 diabetes. Curr Diab Rep, 2010. **10**(2): p. 152-8.
17. Murtaugh, M.A., et al., Epidemiological support for the protection of whole-grains against diabetes. Proc Nutr Soc, 2003. **62**(1): p. 143-9.
18. Amini, M., et al., People with impaired glucose tolerance and impaired fasting glucose are similarly susceptible to cardiovascular disease: a study in first-degree relatives of type 2 diabetic patients. Ann Nutr Metab, 2010. **56**(4): p. 267-72.
19. Nicholson, A.S., et al., Toward improved management of NIDDM: A randomized, controlled, pilot intervention using a lowfat, vegetarian diet. Prev Med, 1999. **29**(2): p. 87-91.
20. Barnard, N.D., et al., A low-fat vegan diet improves glycemic control and cardiovascular risk factors in a randomized clinical trial in individuals with type 2 diabetes. Diabetes Care, 2006. **29**(8): p. 1777-83.
21. Barnard, N.D., et al., A low-fat vegan diet and a conventional diabetes diet in the treatment of type 2 diabetes: a randomized, controlled, 74-wk clinical trial. Am J Clin Nutr, 2009. **89**(5): p. 1588S-1596S.
22. De Natale, C., et al., Effects of a plant-based high-carbohydrate/high-fiber diet versus high-monounsaturated fat/low-carbohydrate diet on postprandial lipids in type 2 diabetic patients. Diabetes Care, 2009. **32**(12): p. 2168-73.
23. Stephenson, T.J., et al., Effect of soy protein-rich diet on renal function in young adults with insulin-dependent diabetes mellitus. Clin Nephrol, 2005. **64**(1): p. 1-11.
24. Weickert, M.O., et al., Cereal fiber improves whole-body insulin sensitivity in overweight and obese women. Diabetes Care, 2006. **29**(4): p. 775-80.

25. Behall, K.M., et al., Consumption of both resistant starch and beta-glucan improves post-prandial plasma glucose and insulin in women. Diabetes Care, 2006. **29**(5): p. 976-81.

26. Jang, Y., et al., Consumption of whole-grain and legume powder reduces insulin demand, lipid peroxidation, and plasma homocysteine concentrations in patients with coronary artery disease: randomized controlled clinical trial. Arterioscler Thromb Vasc Biol, 2001. **21**(12): p. 2065-71.

27. Rave, K., et al., Improvement of insulin resistance after diet with a whole-grain based dietary product: results of a randomized, controlled cross-over study in obese subjects with elevated fasting blood glucose. Br J Nutr, 2007. **98**(5): p. 929-36.

28. Jenkins, D.J., et al., Type 2 diabetes and the vegetarian diet. Am J Clin Nutr, 2003. **78**(3 Suppl): p. 610S-616S.

07

Chapter 07

Plant-Based Eating and Healthy Bones

Summary

- Achieving optimum bone health during childhood and adolescence is not only important during this period, but it is also key in keeping bones healthy throughout life.
- To ensure bone health throughout life, the World Health Organisation (WHO) recommend that it's important to: achieve the highest possible bone mass during the time of growth, maintain bone health in early adulthood and reduce the rate of bone loss in later life.
- A healthy lifestyle to maintain bone health is encouraged for all, from young to old.
- A varied and adequate diet with increased consumption of fruits, vegetables, legumes, whole-grains and nuts and regular weight bearing physical activity are important components of this healthy lifestyle.
- Evidence from observational studies indicates those who follow plant-based eating have a healthy bone mass.
- Greater fruit and vegetable consumption may make a positive contribution to good bone health.
- Specific plant foods, such as those containing soya isoflavones, may help to reduce bone loss in later life.
- A more alkaline diet, rich in fruit and vegetable intake and with lower consumption of meat, reduces the acid/base challenge that can result in minerals, such as calcium being leached out of bones.

Facts about Bone

Bone is a living tissue which is constantly being renewed by two types of cells. One type builds up new bone (bone formation) and the other breaks down old bone (bone loss). Bone formation and bone loss takes place throughout life, although at different rates at different times. Up to the age of about 30, new bone is made faster than old bone is broken down resulting in an increase in bone mass.

Bone mass is an important indicator of bone strength. While mass is not the only indicator of strength, the relationship between mass, density and strength of bones is important for all ages[1].

Many factors are known to effect bone mass accumulated during growth. Genetic and inherited factors are the major elements that influence bone mass. However gender, dietary components, hormonal factors, physical activity and body weight also have an important role.

Peak bone mass (PBM) or optimal bone mass is when the full genetic potential for bone strength is achieved and it's essential that this is attained in childhood and adolescence. Storing plenty of bone during these years puts the skeleton in a better position to withstand the bone loss that occurs in later years. A number of reviews have made clear associations between PBM attained prior to adulthood and PBM in later life. Higher PBM is associated with a reduced risk of osteoporosis and osteoporotic fractures in later life[1-2].

Challenge of Bone Health in Europe

Poor bone health in Western Societies usually does not manifest itself until later life (unless there are nutrient deficiencies or extreme malnutrition) when the number of fractures, particularly osteoporotic fractures, increases in adults over 50. Osteoporosis or brittle bone disease is defined as a metabolic bone disease that has two principal characteristics: low bone mass and deterioration in the architecture of bone tissue. Both factors lead to enhanced bone fragility and a consequent increase in fracture risk. Onset of osteoporosis occurs in women and men over 50 years, although it can also affect younger women and men too.

Worldwide variation in the incidence and prevalence of osteoporosis is difficult to determine because of problems with definition and diagnosis. The most useful way of comparing osteoporosis prevalence between populations is to use fracture rates in older people. However, because osteoporosis is usually not life-threatening, quantitative data from developing countries are scarce. The current consensus is that approximately 1.66 million hip fractures occur each year worldwide and the incidence of fracture is set to increase four-fold by 2050 due to the increasing numbers of older people[3]. Also, the age-adjusted incidence rates are many times higher in affluent developed countries than in less developed regions of the world. In the year 2000, it was estimated that in the WHO European region there were over 3 million osteoporotic fractures representing over one third of the total worldwide[3]. In countries with a high fracture incidence, rates are greater among women by three to four fold. For example, in the UK, one in two women and one in five men over the age of 50 will break a bone, mainly because of poor bone health.

Maintaining Healthy Bones

In order to maximise bone health throughout life, WHO have identified that it is important to:

1. Achieve the highest possible bone mass during the time of growth - childhood through to early adulthood;
2. Maintain bone health in early adulthood; and
3. Reduce the rate of bone loss in later life[4].

In fact, bone health throughout life is highly dependent on PBM status achieved in young adulthood. 90% of peak bone mass occurs by the age of 18 in girls and 20 years in boys (when growth ceases). Bone density continues to increase slowly until people are in their mid to late 20s. At this point the balance between bone loss and bone formation stays stable.

Adequate calcium (Ca) intake and vitamin D status in children and adolescents, is required for optimal bone health throughout the lifecycle[5]. In fact all living cells require Ca to survive, but the majority (99%) of Ca is found in bones and teeth and the remainder in soft tissues and body fluids. Vitamin D is the generic term for two molecules: ergocalciferol (vitamin D2) and cholecalciferol (vitamin D3). Vitamin D2 is derived by ultraviolet (UV) irradiation of ergosterol, which is distributed in plants, fungi, eggs and oily fish whereas vitamin D3 is formed from the effect of UV irradiation on the skin. The principal role of vitamin D is to maintain blood Ca concentration within narrow limits and together these two nutrients are essential for bone health.

FIGURE 7.1 – Peak Bone Mass Achievement throughout Life

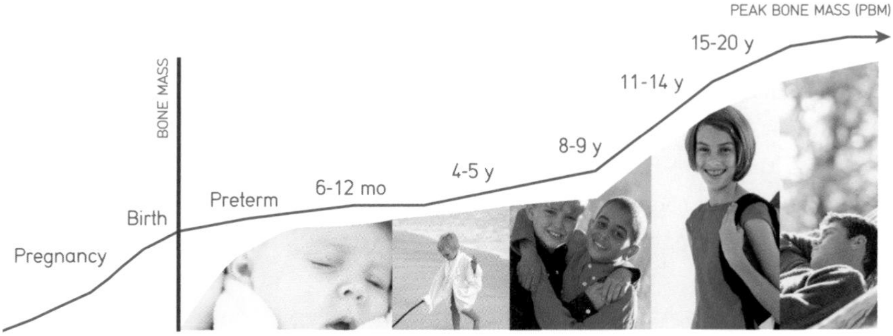

Source: Based on Atkinson SA. McMaster University 2005

Intakes of Ca are a concern among certain groups of the population, for example a high proportion of teenage boys and girls (12%) in the UK fail to meet the lower reference nutrient intake for Ca[6]. For vitamin D, there are no dietary reference values for 4–64 year olds, as it is considered that UV exposure will meet the requirement for this vitamin. However there is increasing evidence of vitamin D inadequacy in certain sectors of the population including those who do not expose their skin to sunlight either for religious or cultural reasons or concerns about skin health.

Chronic Ca deficiency resulting from inadequate intake or poor intestinal absorption is one of several important causes of reduced bone mass and osteoporosis. It is vital, therefore, that adequate dietary Ca is consumed at all stages of life. Besides the amount of Ca in the diet, the absorption of dietary Ca in foods is also a critical factor in determining the availability of Ca for bone development and maintenance.

Modifiable dietary and lifestyle factors will influence whether the genetic potential for PBM is achieved. Key interventions that can be made, which are vital determinants of BMD, are physical activity, calcium intake, and vitamin D stores (from sunlight conversion of precursors of vitamin D and from dietary intake)[1,7]. Adequate protein intake and an appropriate energy intake are also important factors.

The WHO guidelines for diet are appropriate recommendations for promoting bone health; it is recommended that populations and individuals should aim to:

- achieve energy balance and a healthy weight (physical activity is a key determinant of energy expenditure, and thus is fundamental to energy balance and weight control);

- limit energy intake from total fats and shift fat consumption away from saturated fats to unsaturated fats and towards the elimination of *trans* fatty acids;
- increase consumption of fruits and vegetables, and legumes, whole-grains and nuts;
- limit the intake of sugars and limit salt (sodium) consumption from all sources and ensure that salt is iodized[8].

Other nutrients and dietary factors, for example protein intake, may be important for long-term bone health and the prevention of osteoporosis. Specifically many of the essential micronutrients have been suggested to be involved with skeletal health including, zinc, copper, manganese, boron, vitamin A, vitamin C, vitamin K, the B vitamins, potassium and sodium[15]. However evidence from physiological and clinical studies is largely lacking and the data is often difficult to interpret.

The WHO has identified that physical activity is also important for bone health, and has suggested that:

1. Children and youths aged 5–17 should undertake at least 60 minutes of moderate-to vigorous-intensity physical activity daily.
2. Physical activity greater than 60 minutes provides additional health benefits.
3. Most of the daily physical activity should be aerobic. Vigorous-intensity activities should also be incorporated, including those that strengthen muscle and bone, at least 3 times per week.

It has been further suggested that the benefits of being physically active outweigh any potential harms. Any existing risk can be reduced by gradually increasing activity level, especially in children and young people who are inactive.

WHO have summarised the strength of evidence linking diet to osteoporotic fractures, see Table 7.1[9].

TABLE 7.1 – Summary of Strength of Evidence Linking Diet to Osteoporotic Fractures

Evidence	Decreased risk	No relationship	Increased risk
Convincing Older People[a]	Vitamin D Calcium Physical activity		High alcohol intake Low body weight
Probable Older People[a]		Fluoride[b]	
Possible	Fruits and vegetables[c] Moderate alcohol intake Soy products	Phosphorus	High sodium intake Low protein intake (in older people) High protein intake

a: In populations with high fracture incidence only. Applies to men and women older than 50-60 years, with a low calcium intake and/or poor vitamin D status.

b: At levels used to fluoridate water supplies. High fluoride intake causes fluorosis and may also alter bone matrix.

c: Several components of fruits and vegetables are associated with a decreased risk at levels of intake within the normal range of consumption (e.g. alkalinity, vitamin K, phytoestrogens, potassium, magnesium, boron) Vitamin C deficiency (scurvy) results in osteopenic bone disease.

Potential Benefits of Plant-Based Eating

There are possible benefits of fruit and vegetable consumption for bone health as identified by WHO (see Table 7.1). Also important for bone health is the need to maintain a healthy body weight and active lifestyle, which tends to be found in those consuming vegetarian or plant-based eating as discussed in Chapter 05.

Nevertheless, there has been concern expressed that moving towards a plant-based eating regime would result in deficiencies in particular nutrients, specifically protein, zinc, iron, Vitamin B12, Vitamin D and calcium[10-12]. However a review that considered the evidence for this concluded that this needn't be the case and suggested that based on the evidence, meat is an optional rather than an essential constituent of human diets[13]. Despite this opinion, there is no doubt that many people will be concerned about the adequacy of plant-based eating to provide sufficient calcium due to the strong link between calcium and dairy foods. While the nutrient adequacy of plant-based eating has been discussed in detail in Chapter 02, the findings related to calcium intake and bone health specifically will be further discussed below.

Scientific Evidence

In this area, observational studies can provide information about dietary patterns and BMD or bone mineral content (BMC) over time. These studies provide the majority of evidence relating to diet and bone health. Because bone growth and development occurs over a long period of time, short term RCTs are relatively few in number in this area of research and often can only address aspects of diet and markers of bone growth, turnover, or loss of bone. Longer term RCT's generally are conducted in postmenopausal women and may, by using x-ray techniques, measure bone loss over time. However ideally these studies should be a minimum of two years duration and, as such, are expensive to conduct and consequently are again few in number.

Observational Studies

The majority of the observational studies measure an association between lacto-vegetarian, vegetarian or vegan diets and a measure of bone health usually BMD or BMC. An additional complication is that bone health is measured at a number of sites, for example, generally BMD or BMC are measured in bones from the spine, hip or leg, but it may also be bone from the arm or wrist. As the various bones grow and turnover at different rates, it is only valid to make comparisons between measurements taken at the same site.

In a recent review of the literature, data from nine observational studies were pooled and subject to a Bayesian-type meta-analysis[14]. This type of analysis looks at the probability of treatment effect and as such does not provide the "conclusive" evidence that public health specialists require. The reviewed studies all measured BMD at either, or both, the lumbar spine or femoral neck (base of the head of the leg bone). A weakness of this analysis is that it contained data from five studies where the subjects were Asian and only four studies relating to white populations. Overall subject numbers were low with 2749 subjects included in the analysis of which, 1880 were women and 869 were men with a mean age of between 27 to 79 years. The median sample size of the studies was 152 and these were split equally between omnivores and vegetarians. Of the 9 eligible studies, 6 studies were conducted in lacto-ovovegetarians, and 3 in vegans. Overall BMD, at both the femoral neck and the lumbar spine was 4% lower in vegetarians, than in omnivores. Compared with omnivores, vegans had a significantly lower lumbar spine BMD (6% lower) and this was more pronounced than in lacto-ovovegetarians, where lumbar spine BMD was 2% lower. In vegetarians, compared to omnivores, the probability that BMD was 5% or more lower, was 42% for the femoral neck and 32% for the lumbar spine. The authors concluded that these associations were clinically insignificant[14]; a view supported by Dr Lanham-New in an editorial that reviewed the analysis[15]. She concluded that this meta analysis, as well as the findings of the 5-year prospective study of changes in radial bone density in elderly white American women (which showed no differences in bone loss rates between vegetarians and omnivores[16]), demonstrate that vegetarianism is not a serious risk factor for osteoporotic fracture. In addition, she also pointed to additional weaknesses in the analysis, specifically that the results did not fully adjust for key confounding factors, such as for differences in body weight (indeed in half of the studies body weight was significantly lower in the vegetarian group compared with the omnivore group). This is important as it is well established that body weight is a key determinant of bone mineral density. Physical activity levels and smoking, as well as the considerable differences in genetic-ethnic backgrounds in the population studied (Asian compared with white) were also not fully adjusted.

Included in this meta analysis, but worthy of mention in its own right, is the data from the European Prospective Investigation into Cancer and Nutrition (EPIC)-Oxford cohort[17]. Data from 7947 men and 26,749 women aged 20-89 years, including 19,249 meat eaters, 4901 fish eaters, 9420 vegetarians and 1126 vegans, were monitored for an average of 5.2 years. During this time 343 men and 1555 women reported one or more fractures. Compared with meat eaters, fracture incidence rate ratios in men and women, adjusted for sex, age and non-dietary factors, were 1.01 for fish eaters, 1.00 for vegetarians and 1.30 for vegans. These results suggest that only the vegans had a 30% greater risk of fracture (although this was non-significant). This was halved to 15% after adjustment for dietary energy and calcium intake. Among subjects consuming at least 525 mg of calcium a day the corresponding incidence rate ratios were 1.05 for fish eaters, 1.02 for vegetarians and 1.00 for vegans, indicating that the higher fracture risk in the vegans appeared to be a consequence of their considerably lower mean calcium intake. An adequate calcium intake is essential for bone health, irrespective of dietary preferences.

Observational studies not included in this meta-analysis include data from the first and second Adventist Health Studies that included 1865 peri- and post-menopausal women of which a significant proportion consumed a meat-free diet. These women completed two lifestyle surveys 25 years apart and this was used to evaluate the effects of foods high in protein on the risk of wrist fracture[18]. The study found there was a significant interaction between meat consumption and foods high in vegetable protein on the risk of wrist fracture. Among vegetarians, those who consumed the least vegetable protein were at highest risk of fracture. However, increasing levels of plant-based high-protein foods decreased wrist fracture risk, with a 68% reduction in risk in the highest intake group. Conversely among those with lowest vegetable protein consumption, increasing meat intake decreased the risk of wrist fracture, with the highest consumption decreasing risk by 80%. Overall higher consumption frequencies of foods rich in protein were associated with reduced wrist fracture and provide evidence to support the importance of adequate protein for bone health. The similarity in risk reduction by vegetable protein foods compared with meat intake suggests that adequate protein intake is attainable in a vegetarian diet.

The EPIC-Oxford cohort has also been used to study the relationship between vitamin D status and risk of fracture. A case-control study, was established within the overall cohort that examined the association between plasma 25-hydroxyvitamin D concentration and fracture risk among more than 2,000 adults in the United Kingdom[19]. Dietary intake of vitamin D and diet group were strongly associated with plasma levels. However, overall the proportion of variation in plasma 25-hydroxyvitamin D levels explained by dietary intake was very low at 4.5% in men and 1.2% women and exposure to sunlight was of much greater importance. Vegans had the lowest level of 25-hydroxyvitamin D, reflecting their lower intake of vitamin D. The major determinant of 25-hydroxyvitamin D in this population was age and exposure to ultraviolet radiation. Overall there was no evidence of an association between plasma 25-hydroxyvitamin D and fracture risk for men or women.

An earlier review of the literature relating to vegetarian diets and bone mass included evidence related to observational, clinical and intervention studies[20]. Studies were reviewed by date of publication pre-1984 and post-1984. From the seven identified studies published pre-1984 it was concluded that BMD was higher in those following a vegetarian diet, although many of the identified studies were conducted in Seventh Day Adventists who have many lifestyle features that differ from the population at large. There were fewer post-1984 observational studies - five were identified and these showed no real consistent effect of a vegetarian diet on BMD. Overall the key findings were that there was no difference in bone health indices between lacto-ovovegetarians and omnivores, and that vegetarians appear to have a normal bone mass. There was conflicting data for protein effects on bone, and growing support for a beneficial effect of fruit and vegetable intake on bone health[20]. In addition the review identified the complexities of evaluating the role of vegetarian diets on bone health due to the interaction of various dietary components such as calcium, protein, acid/alkali-balance, vitamins D and K as well as specific functional components, such as isoflavones from soya foods.

Another aspect that can be investigated as a marker of bone health is the acid-base load of the diet. Evidence exists that a diet that increases the acidity of blood and other body fluids may result in minerals, including Ca, being leached out of bones which would be detrimental to bone health. The relationship between urine pH and dietary acid-base load, and its contributory food groups (fruit and vegetables, meats, cereal and dairy foods), was investigated in 22,034 men and women aged 39-78 years living in Norfolk (UK) using dietary intakes from the EPIC-Norfolk food frequency questionnaire (FFQ)[21]. From this study, data from 363 volunteers was used to compare urinary pH and 24 h urine output with dietary intakes from a 7-day diary and the FFQ. A more alkaline diet, which had a high fruit and vegetable intake and lower consumption of meat, was significantly associated with a more alkaline urine pH. This was before and after adjustment for age, BMI, physical activity and smoking habit and also after excluding for urinary protein, glucose, ketones, diagnosed high blood pressure and diuretic medication. The effects of a more alkaline diet, higher in fruit and vegetables and lower in meat intake, were related to more alkaline urine with an effect similar to that reported in intervention studies investigating acid-base diets.

Intervention Studies

Intervention studies are often used to assess bone turnover by measuring a number of different markers. A slight variation on this approach assessed calcium balance of individuals on a vegan diet in comparison with a lacto-vegetarian diet[22]. Seven women and one man, aged 19 to 24 years, received a vegan diet based on plant foods and calcium-rich mineral water for the first 10 days and a lacto-vegetarian diet during the following 10 days. Calcium status was assessed by means of calcium intake in food and calcium output in faeces and urine. Deoxypyridinoline was measured in urine as a marker of bone resorption (break-down). The results show a significantly lower average daily calcium intake in the vegan phase (843 ± 140mg) compared to 1322 ± 303mg in the lacto-vegetarian phase. Apparent calcium absorption rates were calculated as 26% ± 15% and 24% ± 8% in the vegan and lacto-vegetarian phases respectively. The calcium balance was positive and not significantly different in the vegan (119 ± 113mg/day) and lacto-vegetarian phase (211 ± 136mg/day). Deoxypyridinoline excretion was also not significantly different between the two diet phases. This short term study indicates that calcium balance and a marker of bone turnover are not significantly affected when calcium is provided either solely by plant foods and calcium enriched water, or by a diet including dairy products, despite the significantly different calcium intake levels. This study also highlights how a well-selected vegan diet maintains calcium status, at least for a short-term period.

It has been suggested that specific plant foods may have a beneficial effect on bone health in later life. Of these, soya is the most promising and extensively researched. There is a large group of intervention studies that have evaluated the role of soya isoflavones on reducing bone loss in postmenopausal women and this data has been recently reviewed[23]. Data from ten eligible RCTs conducted in 896 women for at least a year, were pooled and a meta-analysis conducted. A mean dose of 87 mg soya isoflavones for at least one year did not significantly affect BMD changes. The mean differences in BMD changes were 4.1mg/cm^2 per year equivalent to 0.4% difference at the lumbar spine, -1.5mg/cm^2 or -0.3% at the femoral neck and 2.5 mg/cm^2 or 0.2% at the total hip. The results were similar when the analysis was conducted by source of isoflavones either, soya protein containing foods or isoflavone extract. At higher rates of inclusion (≥ 80 mg isoflavones/day compared to < 80mg/day), there was a beneficial, but non-significant effect on BMD ($P = 0.08$)[23]. In a second meta analysis, conducted with 10 studies and a total of 608 subjects, followed for a minimum of 6 months, spine BMD in subjects who consumed isoflavones increased significantly by 20.6 mg/cm^2 in comparison to subjects who did not consume isoflavones[24]. In this analysis BMC also increased by 0.93g, which was of borderline significance. The increase in spine BMD achieved with an isoflavone intake of > 90 mg/day was higher at 28.5mg/cm^2. The authors concluded that the addition of isoflavones to the diet significantly attenuates bone loss of the spine in menopausal women and that these favourable effects become more significant when intakes of isoflavones are more than 90 mg/day and the effect can become apparent after 6 months consumption[24].

Overview and Conclusions

The data, primarily from observational studies, indicates that there appears to be nothing inherent in plant-based eating patterns that has an adverse effect on bone health. In fact, emerging evidence would seem to suggest that there may be a beneficial effect related to the greater consumption of fruit and vegetables[25]. There appears to be little difference in bone mass between omnivore and vegetarian populations, particularly those who consume some dairy and fish. However, it appears that for those consuming vegan-type diets care should be taken to preserve protein and calcium intake, particularly during adolescence and young adulthood when peak bone mass is attained. There are a wide variety of plant-based protein sources including peas, beans, lentils, nuts, nut butters (peanut butter), seeds, soya dairy alternatives (soya milk, soya yoghurts), tofu, soya nuts, soya mince, soya sausages etc that can be consumed to ensure protein intakes are maintained. These days the majority of dairy alternatives (soya milks, yoghurts, drinks etc) are fortified with calcium ensuring that calcium requirements can be met from these products. Furthermore calcium is found in fruit and vegetable sources such as dried fruits (e.g. apricots and figs), nuts, green leafy vegetables (especially Kale and Pak-Choi, but not spinach), sesame seeds and tahini.

Plant-based eating tends to be associated with other beneficial lifestyle factors, including greater physical activity, less smoking and overall a lower energy dense and nutrient-rich diet, all of which contribute to good bone health.

Plant-based eating supports normal bone growth and development throughout life provided a wide variety of plant foods are consumed.

Plant-based eating is associated with other lifestyle factors known to be beneficial to bone health such as greater physical activity and being less overweight.

Greater fruit and vegetable consumption may make a positive contribution to good bone health.

Specific plant foods, such as those containing soya isoflavones, may help to reduce bone loss in later life.

Literature chapter 07

1. Heaney, R.P., et al., Peak bone mass. Osteoporos Int, 2000. **11**(12): p. 985-1009.
2. Heaney, R.P. and C.M. Weaver, Newer perspectives on calcium nutrition and bone quality. J Am Coll Nutr, 2005. **24**(6 Suppl): p. 574S-81S.
3. World Health Organization (WHO), WHO Scientific Group on the Assessment of Osteoporosis at Primary Health Care Level, in Summary Meeting Report 5-7 May 2004. 2004, WHO: Brussels, Belgium.
4. World Health Organization (WHO), Study Group on Assessment of Fracture Risk and Its Application to Screening and Postmenopausal Osteoporosis. Report of a WHO Study Group, in Technical Report Series (No. 84) 1994, WHO: Geneva.
5. Cashman, K.D., Vitamin D in childhood and adolescence. Postgrad Med J, 2007. **83**(978): p. 230-5.
6. Lanham-New S, et al., Review: Importance of vitamin D, calcium and exercise to bone health with specific reference to children and adolescents. British Nutrition Foundation, Nutrition Bulletin, 2007. **Dec 2007**(32): p. 364–377.
7. *Nutrition and bone health: with particular reference to calcium and vitamin D. Report of the Subgroup on Bone Health, Working Group on the Nutritional Status of the Population of the Committee on Medical Aspects of the Fo*od Nutrition Policy. Rep Health Soc Subj (Lond), 1998. **49**: p. iii-xvii, 1-24.
8. WHO, 5.2 Recommendations for preventing excess weight gain and obesity, p61-71. 2003, www.who.org.
9. Prentice, A., Diet, nutrition and the prevention of osteoporosis. Public Health Nutr, 2004. **7**(1A): p. 227-43.
10. Freeland-Graves, J., Mineral adequacy of vegetarian diets. Am J Clin Nutr, 1988. **48**(3 Suppl): p. 859-62.
11. Draper, A., et al., The energy and nutrient intakes of different types of vegetarian: a case for supplements? Br J Nutr, 1993. **69**(1): p. 3-19.
12. Dwyer, J.T., Nutritional consequences of vegetarianism. Annu Rev Nutr, 1991. **11**: p. 61-91.
13. Sanders, T.A., The nutritional adequacy of plant-based diets. Proc Nutr Soc, 1999. **58**(2): p. 265-9.
14. Ho-Pham, L.T., N.D. Nguyen, and T.V. Nguyen, Effect of vegetarian diets on bone mineral density: a Bayesian meta-analysis. Am J Clin Nutr, 2009. **90**(4): p. 943-50.
15. Lanham-New, S.A., Is "vegetarianism" a serious risk factor for osteoporotic fracture? Am J Clin Nutr, 2009. **90**(4): p. 910-1.
16. Reed, J.A., et al., Comparative changes in radial-bone density of elderly female lacto-ovovegetarians and omnivores. Am J Clin Nutr, 1994. **59**(5 Suppl): p. 1197S-1202S.
17. Appleby, P., et al., Comparative fracture risk in vegetarians and nonvegetarians in EPIC-Oxford. Eur J Clin Nutr, 2007. **61**(12): p. 1400-6.
18. Thorpe, D.L., et al., Effects of meat consumption and vegetarian diet on risk of wrist fracture over 25 years in a cohort of peri- and postmenopausal women. Public Health Nutr, 2008. **11**(6): p. 564-72.
19. Roddam, A.W., et al., Association between plasma 25-hydroxyvitamin D levels and fracture risk: the EPIC-Oxford study. Am J Epidemiol, 2007. **166**(11): p. 1327-36.
20. New, S.A., Do vegetarians have a normal bone mass? Osteoporos Int, 2004. **15**(9): p. 679-88.
21. Welch, A.A., et al., Urine pH is an indicator of dietary acid-base load, fruit and vegetables and meat intakes: results from the European Prospective Investigation into Cancer and Nutrition (EPIC)-Norfolk population study. Br J Nutr, 2008. **99**(6): p. 1335-43.
22. Kohlenberg-Mueller, K. and L. Raschka, Calcium balance in young adults on a vegan and lactovegetarian diet. J Bone Miner Metab, 2003. **21**(1): p. 28-33.
23. Liu, J., et al., Effect of long-term intervention of soy isoflavones on bone mineral density in women: a meta-analysis of randomized controlled trials. Bone, 2009. **44**(5): p. 948-53.
24. Ma, D.F., et al., Soy isoflavone intake increases bone mineral density in the spine of menopausal women: meta-analysis of randomized controlled trials. Clin Nutr, 2008. **27**(1): p. 57-64.
25. New, S.A., Intake of fruit and vegetables: implications for bone health. Proc Nutr Soc, 2003. **62**(4): p. 889-99.

08

Chapter 08

Plant-Based Eating and Ageing

Summary

- Western populations are living longer resulting in a significant increase in the proportion of older people in society.
- Energy balance is a significant issue in older people; in some there is a risk of inadequate energy intake, but over-nutrition resulting in obesity is becoming more prevalent, however there is convincing evidence that vegetarians have a lower prevalence of obesity.
- The diet of older people is often low in fibre and some micronutrients which can be found in plant foods.
- Attention needs to be focussed on ensuring adequate intakes of calcium, vitamin B12 and D, which may be below the recommended amounts in older people.
- Plant-based eating is associated with a healthier blood cholesterol profile, specifically lower LDL cholesterol, lower rates of coronary heart disease and probably lower rates of hypertension and diabetes.
- Studies indicate that people consuming more plant foods tend to have a lower saturated fat intake and this may be one of the reasons that LDL-cholesterol is lowered, but there are a variety of other factors intrinsic to plant-based eating which may also be important. Overall greater fruit and vegetable consumption can make a positive contribution to good health and longevity.
- Specific plant foods, such as soya containing isoflavones, may have a beneficial effect on symptoms of the menopause in women and help to reduce bone loss in later life.
- A varied and adequate diet with increased consumption of fruits, vegetables, legumes, whole-grains and nuts, as well as regular physical activity, are important components of a healthy lifestyle for older people.

An Ageing Population

The number of individuals aged 60 years or more is escalating rapidly worldwide. The United Nations Population Division estimated that in 1999 this age group represented *ca* 10% of the world's population, or *ca* 600 million people. By 2050, its projected this proportion will double to 20% representing *ca* 2 billion people[1]. In Europe, 20% of the population is already aged 60 years or older with Greece and Italy having the highest proportion of older people (24% in both countries in 2000)[2]. Furthermore it's predicted that the population aged 80 or older will more than triple by 2050 and in addition the number of centurions is expected to increase 15-fold during this time. In virtually all countries women comprise the majority of the older population, largely because globally women live longer than men[2].

The implications of these demographic changes are significant, as there is great potential through healthy lifestyles, which include physical activity, nutritious diets and avoidance of smoking, to promote a long and healthy life.

The specific health issues that face the older population are:

- maintaining weight within the desirable range;
- ensuring bone health, particularly as the majority of the population are women, who after the menopause are most likely to suffer an osteoporotic fracture;
- the challenge of chronic disease, with the most prevalent cause of death in this population being cardiovascular disease (CVD).

Nutritional Needs

Older people are particularly vulnerable to malnutrition and have unique nutrient needs. In the USA, the dietary reference intakes (DRI) recognise two categories of older people with the "greater than age 50 y" split into the 51–70 year olds and > 70 years. This older age group is particularly vulnerable to poor nutrient status[3]. Traditionally, food intake tends to decrease with advancing age to compensate for the diminished energy needs associated with lower energy expended in physical activity and basal metabolic rate. However vitamin and mineral needs either remain constant or increase.

Nutritional concerns for older adults are related to both under and over consumption of energy and nutrients. Attempts to provide adequate nutrition encounter many practical problems. Firstly, nutritional requirements are not well defined; and secondly, their reduced food intake and lack of variety of the foods in their diet can lead to micronutrient deficiencies. For others excess energy intake, either in old- age or during their life time, increases the risk of becoming obese.

The USA has led the way in producing advice targeted at older people and in 1995 developed the Modified Food Guide Pyramid for US adults aged 70+ years[3]. In 2005 this was developed further, although it continues to be based on the principles of the US Dietary Guidelines for Americans and those of other health organisations, such as the WHO. It emphasises that diets should be high in fruits, vegetables, whole-grains, low- and non fat dairy products, legumes, fish, and lean meats, see Figure 8.1[3]. In addition the Pyramid makes reference to the need to promote fluid intake in older people by reference to the row of glasses, which act as a reminder of the need for regular fluid intake. A second row depicts a variety of physical activities to emphasize the importance of regular

FIGURE 8.1 – My Pyramid for Older Adults 2005

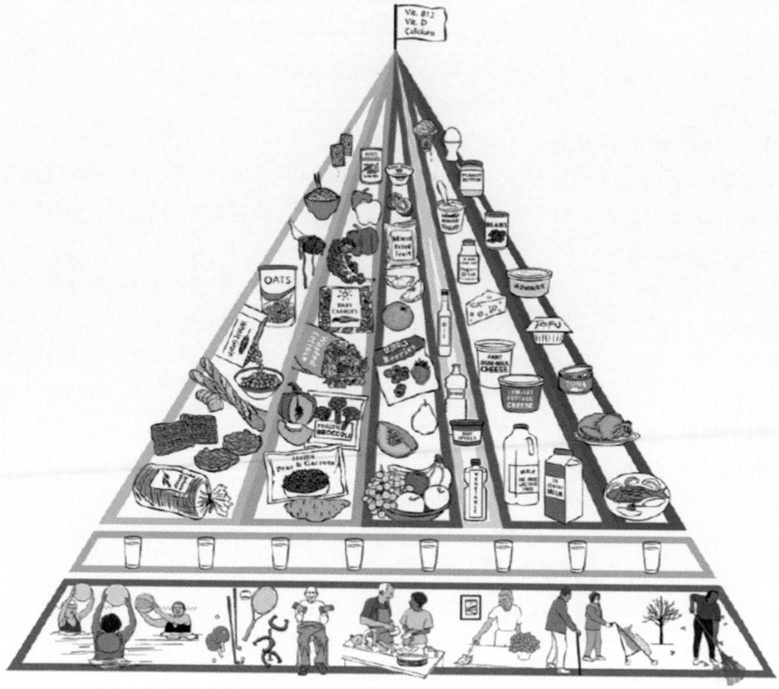

physical activity for this age group. The flag at the top makes reference to vitamins B_{12} and D and calcium - the nutrients most likely to be compromised in the over 70 year olds, and highlights the need to consider an appropriate supplement. At the same time it has been recognised that this group of people are among the highest supplement takers in the population and risk over consumption of other micronutrients specifically folate and sodium[3].

In 2002, the WHO issued, "Keeping Fit for Life", which, using the food-based dietary guideline approach, included the following main lifestyle recommendations for older people[4]:

- Emphasize healthy traditional vegetable- and legume-based dishes.
- Limit traditional dishes/foods that are heavily preserved/ pickled in salt and encourage the use of herbs and spices.
- Introduce healthy traditional foods or dishes from other cuisines (e.g. tofu in Europe and the tomato in Asia).
- Select nutrient-dense foods such as fish, lean meat, liver, eggs, soya products (e.g. tofu and tempeh) and low-fat dairy products, yeast-based products (e.g. spreads), fruits and vegetables, herbs and spices, whole-grain cereals, nuts and seeds.
- Consume fat from whole foods such as nuts, seeds, beans, olives and fatty fish. Where refined fats are necessary for cooking, select from a variety of liquid oils, including those high in omega-3 and omega-9 fats. Avoid fatty spreads.
- Enjoy food and eating in the company of others. Avoid the regular use of celebratory foods (e.g. ice cream, cakes and pastries in western culture, confectioneries and candies in Malay culture, and crackling pork in Chinese culture).
- Encourage the food industry and fast-food chains to produce ready-made meals that are low in animal fats.
- Eat several (5–6) small non-fatty meals. This pattern appears to be associated with greater food variety and lower body fat and blood glucose and lipid levels, especially if larger meals are eaten early in the day.
- Transfer as much as possible of one's food culture, health knowledge and related skills to one's children, grandchildren and the wider community.
- Be physically active on a regular basis and include exercises that strengthen muscles and improve balance.
- Avoid dehydration by regularly consuming, especially in warm climates, fluids and foods with a high water content.

Potential Nutritional Benefits of Plant-Based Eating

It can be seen from the WHO guidance that there is an emphasis on meeting nutritional needs from plant foods and indeed, the trial and consumption of a wider range of plant foods is encouraged. The importance of eating a wide range of foods is particularly relevant in older people consuming plant-based eating patterns, as care should be taken to ensure adequate calcium, vitamin B_{12} and vitamin D intake in later life. Dietary vitamin D assumes greater importance in older people as their exposure to sunlight may be less and the efficiency of the skin to synthesize vitamin D declines with age. In addition, with increasing rates of overweight and obesity in the older population, there is a further concern for vitamin D inadequacy due to its deposition in body fat compartments leading to reduced bioavailability[3]. Ensuring adequate calcium intake in plant-based eating patterns has been discussed in detail in Chapter 02, where mention is made of the wide range of calcium containing plant foods available that can meet calcium needs without increasing saturated fat intake, particularly important for this group of people.

Other micronutrients whose intake may be compromised in older people are vitamins E and K, and potassium. Vegetables and fruits are good sources of these nutrients and consequently plant-based eating can help ensure that their intake is maintained.

It has previously been identified that plant-based eating patterns tend to be rich in fibre (see Chapter 02). This is another important aspect of an older person' diet as it aids laxation. However, typically fibre intake in this age group is lower than is desirable. Data from the UK National Diet and Nutrition Survey of people aged 65 years and over, indicates that fibre intake in men is typically only three quarters of the recommended population intake, and in women of ≥ 65 years it is 60% of recommended levels; clearly both would benefit from the inclusion of more fibre-rich plant foods in the diet[5].

Potential Main Health Benefits of Plant-Based Eating

In Western societies throughout life there is a tendency for people to "put on weight". Not surprisingly overweight and obesity are among the most common nutrition-related disorders in older people. For example, in England, obesity is most prevalent in the 45-75 year olds, affecting around 30% of this population. This reduces in the over 75 year olds to around 20% of this population[6]. Plant-based eating is associated with lower body weight and leaner body mass as discussed in Chapter 05, Consequently in an ageing population this way of eating is a major benefit. Not only is the benefit a healthy body weight, but it also reduces the risk of certain chronic diseases as obesity is a major risk factor for CVD, diabetes and cancer.

Chronic disease is clearly a major consideration for an ageing population. However it appears that while dietary changes seem to affect risk-factor levels throughout life, there may be an even greater impact in older people. Elevated blood cholesterol, a risk factor for CHD in both men and women, is common in older people and this relationship persists into very old age. Relatively modest reductions in saturated fat and salt intake, which would reduce blood pressure and cholesterol concentrations, can have a substantial effect on reducing CVD. It has been suggested by WHO that increasing consumption of fruit and vegetables by one to two servings daily could cut cardiovascular risk by 30%[2].

A further challenge to older people is maintaining bone health and the inclusion of certain soya foods that contain isoflavones appear to have a small beneficial effect in this respect. In addition, women during the menopause may benefit from reduced menopausal symptoms, such as hot flushes, by the inclusion of soya in their diet.

Scientific Evidence

In this area, observational studies can provide information about dietary patterns and the incidence of chronic disease, or cause of death, and thereby indicate which dietary patterns are associated with better health. Other observational data relates specific plant foods, or categories of plant foods, to chronic disease or cause of death. However this data can be difficult to interpret as there are many other variables in people's overall diet and lifestyle and it is not always possible to adjust for all these factors.

Clinical studies provide short and medium term data that usually relate the consumption of a specific plant food to some aspect of ageing for example, bone health, menopausal symptoms, cognitive function and disease risk factors.

Observational Studies

The evidence related to the health effects of vegetarian diets was recently reviewed by Fraser[7]. Although the amount of data outside of the various Adventist cohorts is limited, the author nevertheless concluded that there is convincing evidence that vegetarians have:

1. lower rates of CHD, largely as a result of lower LDL cholesterol,
2. probable evidence of lower rates of hypertension and diabetes mellitus,
3. lower prevalence of obesity,

as described in Table 8.1[7]. In this table the non-vegetarian group is used to establish the baseline risk for hypertension and diabetes, which is given a risk of 1 or 100%. The risk of these chronic diseases reduces in all those adopting vegetarian diets, with the lowest risk being observed among vegans. In this group the risk for hypertension or diabetes respectively is 75 or 78% lower than that of a non-vegetarian.

TABLE 8.1 – Mean Difference in BMI and the Prevalence of Hypertension and Diabetes in Different Types of Vegetarians Compared with Non Vegetarians in California Seventh-Day Adventists·

Diet Group	Body Mass Index· (BMI) kg/m··	Relative prevalence of Hypertension	Relative prevalence of Diabetes
Non vegetarian	28.3	1.00	1.00
Semi-vegetarian	27.0	0.77	0.72
Pesco-vegetarian	25.7	0.62	0.49
Lacto-ovovegetarian	25.5	0.45	0.39
Vegan	23.1	0.25	0.22
Statistical significance (P)	0.0001	0.0001	0.0001

· Number in study = 89,224.
·· Normal weight is classified as BMI <25kg/m^2
Source: Fraser, 2009[7]

Aside from the Californian studies of Adventists, a small number of other cohorts have studied vegetarians and the risk of chronic diseases. These include the UK Health Food Shoppers' Study, the Oxford Vegetarian Study (UK) and the Heidelberg Vegetarian Study in Germany. These studies observed deaths only and, as they were relatively small studies, the number of coronary events was moderate. Nevertheless they indicated a reduction in coronary death, although the position was not as clear cut for cancers at a specific site. The author identified that this appears to be where the conflict in the data on cancer exists - specifically with regard to colorectal cancer - which was reduced in the Adventist studies, but increased in the European Prospective Investigation into Cancer and Nutrition (EPIC-Oxford) cohort.

The mortality data of vegetarians and non-vegetarians was collected from the EPIC-Oxford cohort which included 64,234 subjects, aged 20-89 years, and for whom diet group was known. By 30 June 2007, 2965 subjects had died before the age of 90. The death rates of participants were much lower than the United Kingdom average and were identical in vegetarians and in non vegetarians. In a sub set of 47,254 people who did not have CVD or cancer at recruitment, when vegetarians were compared with meat eaters, the adjusted death rate was 19% lower for heart disease and no different for all causes of death[8]. As mentioned above the incidence rate for colorectal cancer in vegetarians compared with meat eaters was 39% higher, although within the study, the incidence of all cancers combined was lower among vegetarians than among meat eaters[9].

Fraser, in trying to explain the difference between the Adventist and EPIC cohort, has suggested that perhaps the category of vegetarian is too wide and that its definition by default as a diet without meat, can lead to a wide variation in the actual food groups consumed. There would appear to be a wide variation in the diet consumed by the Californian Adventists and the health-conscious in Oxford, which may well account for the differences between these groups[7].

The possible role of monounsaturated and polyunsaturated fats and other selected food groups in protecting against all-causes mortality were investigated in a population-based study, the Italian Longitudinal Study on Ageing, in Casamassima, Bari, Italy[10]. 278 elderly subjects (aged 65-84 years) with a typical Mediterranean diet, were followed for a mean period of 8.5 years and during this period there were 91 deaths. A semi-quantitative food frequency questionnaire was used to assess nutrient intake. From this it was found that monounsaturated fat intake was associated with a 19% increased survival rate. A higher unsaturated fatty acid to saturated fatty acid ratio increased total mortality only marginally, by *ca* 20%. Unlike other studies, there was no effect of any other selected food groups. Overall in this small study, it was concluded that any effects of their Mediterranean diet were marginal.

The independent roles of saturated fat intake and fruit and vegetable intake on total and CHD mortality was assessed among 501 initially healthy men in the Baltimore Longitudinal Study of Ageing[1]. Over a mean 18 years follow-up, diet records were collected on 1-7 occasions. From these, both fruit and vegetable intake and saturated fat intakes were individually associated with lower all-cause and CHD mortality ($P < 0.05$). Men consuming a combination of ≥ 5 servings of fruit and vegetables /day and ≤ 12% energy from saturated fat were 31% less likely to die of any cause ($P < 0.05$), and 76% less likely to die from CHD ($P < 0.001$), relative to those consuming less than 5 servings of fruit and vegetables and > 12% saturated fat. Men consuming either a low saturated fat or a high fruit and vegetables intake, but not both, did not have a significantly lower risk of total mortality; but did have 64-67% lower risk of CHD mortality ($P < 0.05$) relative to those doing neither.

Higher fruit and vegetable consumption has previously been reported to protect against all cause mortality, see for example, the EPIC Elderly Study in Europe[11]. However the fact that saturated fat modification and greater consumption of fruit and vegetable act independently in reducing the risk of CHD is an interesting development of the data[1]. Perhaps suggesting that plant-based or vegetarian diets can be beneficial with regard to CHD not only because of the greater consumption of fruit and vegetables, but also because of the lower saturated fat intakes associated with these diets[2].

A higher consumption of whole-grain cereals has also been associated with a 21% lower risk of CVD events. The data is derived from a meta analysis conducted by pooling the data from seven cohort studies[12]. Greater whole-grain intake - an average of 2.5 servings/ day vs. 0.2 servings/ day - was also associated with a lower risk of different CVD outcomes, specifically heart disease, stroke or fatal CVD.

Intervention Studies

It has been suggested that specific plant foods, such as soya, may have a beneficial effect on bone health in later life. Evidence relating to soya and bone health was detailed in Chapter 07. It was concluded that the addition of soya isoflavones to the diet seems, on balance, to have a small beneficial effect and bone loss in menopausal women is attenuated. The favourable effects become more significant when intakes of isoflavones are more than 90 mg/day[13]. A further benefit from soya consumption in the ageing female population is the effect it has on menopausal symptoms, such as hot flushes and also on cognitive decline.

With regard to menopausal symptoms and the use of isoflavones there are six meta analyses of randomised controlled clinical studies conducted to date. Of these, poor characterisation of the isoflavone containing food or supplement is evident in some reviews[14-19]. However, specific attention was given to this aspect in one review, and in this, studies were compared on the basis of the quantity of free genistein (the most predominant isoflavone found in soya) consumed[20]. All five studies investigating intakes of 15 mg genistein per treatment in healthy menopausal and breast cancer sufferers, consistently reported a statistically significant decrease in hot flush symptoms[20]. The consensus view of the EU-funded project Phytohealth was also positive, concluding that soya bean isoflavone extracts could be effective in reducing hot flushes, but the effect is about half that observed with HRT and similar to that of other non-hormonal pharmacological therapies[21].

It should be noted that overall menopausal study quality has now improved and it has been suggested on the basis of more recent data that typically hot flushes are reduced by *ca* 20-30% provided a minimum level of *ca* 40-60mg isoflavones/ day is included in the diet. This is equivalent to around 2-3 servings of soya products such as soya milk and yoghurt alternatives, soya nuts or tofu[20].

With regard to cognitive function in postmenopausal women, at this stage there are few available studies, and it is not possible to draw a conclusion on the effect of soya bean foods or isoflavones[21]. Looking more broadly at plant-based or vegetarian diets again there is little data to indicate any benefits or otherwise from consuming these diets on cognitive function in older people. A number of cohort studies have recently been established, but as yet findings of significance have not been reported.

There are extensive clinical trials that have evaluated the effectiveness of specific plant foods in reducing the risk of CVD - the major cause of ill health in older people. Generally these studies measure the effect of short term introduction of the specific food in the diet on blood cholesterol or blood pressure. Plant foods such as those containing beta glucans (oats and barley) soya protein, plant stanols and sterols appear to be effective in reducing blood cholesterol by around 5-10%[22]. For further details see Chapter 04.

Overview and Conclusions

Western populations are living longer with a significant increase in the proportion of older people in society. Currently most Western European countries have over 20% of the population aged 60 years or more and this is predicted to increase further. Plant-based eating is just as relevant to the ageing population as it is to the population at large. It is associated with a lower incidence of obesity, which is beneficial in its own right, but also as it reduces the risk of developing heart disease, diabetes and cancer. Plant-based eating patterns also tend to be rich in micronutrients and fibre, nutrients that can be limiting in the diets of older people. Other nutrients that may be below reference nutrient intakes in the diets of older people are calcium, vitamins B_{12} and D. Care should be taken to ensure adequate supplies of these nutrients are present in the diet by consuming a wide range of plant foods, if necessary choosing foods fortified with these nutrients.

In this ageing population CVD is the main cause of death. Plant-based eating tends to be associated with a lower risk of CVD (as discussed in Chapter 04) and also a lower incidence of death from CVD as detailed in the observational studies above.

A varied and adequate diet with increased consumption of fruits, vegetables, legumes, whole-grains and nuts and regular physical activity are important components of a healthy lifestyle for older people.

Achieving energy balance is important in older people where overweight or obesity may be prevalent; plant-based eating patterns, which tend to be lower in energy and nutrient-rich can help maintain a healthy weight.

Vegetarian diets are associated with a reduced incidence of death from CHD, stroke and diabetes.

Greater fruit and vegetable consumption may make a positive contribution to the health of older people, as can soya foods that may improve bone health and moderate symptoms of the menopause.

A varied diet with increased consumption of fruits, vegetables, legumes, whole-grains and nuts, and adequate intakes of calcium, vitamin B12 and D, as well as regular and physical activity are important components of a healthy lifestyle for older people.

Literature chapter 08

1. Tucker, K.L., et al., *The combination of high fruit and vegetable and low saturated fat intakes is more protective against mortality in aging men than is either alone: the Baltimore Longitudinal Study of Aging.* J Nutr, 2005. **135**(3): p. 556-61.
2. World Health Organization (WHO), *Nutrition for older persons. Ageing and nutrition: a growing global challenge*, in *http://www.who.int/nutrition/topics/ageing/en/index2.html.*
3. Lichtenstein, A.H., et al., *Modified MyPyramid for Older Adults.* J Nutr, 2008. **138**(1): p. 5-11.
4. World Health Organization (WHO), *Keep fit for life. Meeting the nutritional needs of older persons*, 2002, World Health Organization: Geneva, Switerland.
5. Milton, J.E., et al., *Relationship of glycaemic index with cardiovascular risk factors: analysis of the National Diet and Nutrition Survey for people aged 65 and older.* Public Health Nutr, 2007. **10**(11): p. 1321-35.
6. http://www.heartstats.org.uk, in *Body mass index by sex and age, England, Scotland and Wales, latest available year (Table)*, http://www.heartstats.org.uk/temp/Tabsp3.2spdopa06web.xls.
7. Fraser, G.E., *Vegetarian diets: what do we know of their effects on common chronic diseases?* Am J Clin Nutr, 2009. **89**(5): p. 1607S-1612S.
8. Key, T.J., et al., *Mortality in British vegetarians: results from the European Prospective Investigation into Cancer and Nutrition (EPIC-Oxford).* Am J Clin Nutr, 2009. **89**(5): p. 1613S-1619S.
9. Key, T.J., et al., *Cancer incidence in vegetarians: results from the European Prospective Investigation into Cancer and Nutrition (EPIC-Oxford).* Am J Clin Nutr, 2009. **89**(5): p. 1620S-1626S.
10. Solfrizzi, V., et al., *Unsaturated fatty acids intake and all-causes mortality: a 8.5-year follow-up of the Italian Longitudinal Study on Aging.* Exp Gerontol, 2005. **40**(4): p. 335-43.
11. *Trichopoulou, A., et al., Modified Mediterranean diet and survival: EPIC-elderly prospective cohort study.* BMJ, 2005. **330**(7498): p. 991.
12. Mellen, P.B., T.F. Walsh, and D.M. Herrington, *Whole-grain intake and cardiovascular disease: A meta-analysis.* Nutr Metab Cardiovasc Dis, 2007.
13. Ma, D.F., et al., *Soy isoflavone intake increases bone mineral density in the spine of menopausal women: meta-analysis of randomized controlled trials.* Clin Nutr, 2008. **27**(1): p. 57-64.
14. Bolanos-Diaz, R., et al., *Soy extracts versus hormone therapy for reduction of menopausal hot flushes: indirect comparison.* Menopause, 2011.
15. Low Dog, T., *Menopause: a review of botanical dietary supplements.* Am J Med, 2005. **118 Suppl 12B**: p. 98-108.
16. Lethaby, A.E., et al., *Phytoestrogens for vasomotor menopausal symptoms.* Cochrane Database Syst Rev, 2007(4): p. CD001395.
17. Jacobs, A., et al., *Efficacy of isoflavones in relieving vasomotor menopausal symptoms - A systematic review.* Mol Nutr Food Res, 2009. **53**(9): p. 1084-97.
18. Nelson, H.D., et al., *Nonhormonal therapies for menopausal hot flashes: systematic review and meta-analysis.* Jama, 2006. **295**(17): p. 2057-71.
19. Howes, L.G., J.B. Howes, and D.C. Knight, *Isoflavone therapy for menopausal flushes: a systematic review and meta-analysis.* Maturitas, 2006. **55**(3): p. 203-11.
20. Williamson-Hughes, P.S., et al., *Isoflavone supplements containing predominantly genistein reduce hot flash symptoms: a critical review of published studies.* Menopause, 2006. **13**(5): p. 831-9.
21. Cassidy, A., et al., *Critical review of health effects of soyabean phyto-oestrogens in post-menopausal women.* Proc Nutr Soc, 2006. **65**(1): p. 76-92.
22. Harland JI, *A simple method of comparing dietary approaches that reduce saturates, improve fat quality and indicates the likely effect on blood cholesterol*, in *The 79th European Athersclerosis Society Congress, Joint Session with EACPR: Healthy diets and functional food - a road to prevention.* 2011: Gothenburg, Sweden.

09

Chapter 09

Plant-Based Eating and the Environment

Summary

- A growing global population, increasing urbanisation and economic growth are placing a huge demand on worldwide food supplies, especially animal products.
- This global demand, based on current food consumption patterns, is neither sustainable nor feasible as it puts tremendous pressure on the environment.
- Environmental challenges related to food production include changes to land use, climate change and pressures on natural resources such as water and energy supplies.
- There is evidence that plant foods are more sustainable than animal foods requiring less land, water and energy resources and produce fewer greenhouse gas emissions.
- A sustainable diet that is good for the planet, as well as health, requires a change in eating patterns including consuming more plant-based foods and eating fewer meat and dairy products.

Introduction

For many years, dietary messages have mainly focused on the benefits a nutritious diet provides to health. However there is now growing interest on the impact food choices are having on the environment too. The reasons for this are two-fold. Firstly, it's estimated that there will be nine billion people on the planet by 2050[1]. Consequently more food will be required to feed this growing population. Secondly, global dietary patterns are changing – as societies are becoming more affluent there is shift towards a more 'Western' style of eating with a focus on animal products. Due to this there is an increased demand for these animal foods. As a result it has been estimated that global meat demand could double from 251 million tonnes in 2005 to 563 million tonnes by 2050[2]. Currently meat and seafood are the two most rapidly growing ingredients in the global diet – four times as much meat is now being produced compared to 1961[3]. This global food demand is neither sustainable nor feasible as it will place even greater stress on an already limited supply of land and natural resources such as energy and water. Furthermore, it will have a noticeable impact on climate change and biodiversity. All of these factors pose major challenges for food provision and security. In fact, the World Wildlife Fund (WWF) has suggested that we would need two planets by 2050 to support this global food demand.

Clearly what a person chooses to eat can make a big difference to the environment. The good news is that plant-based eating is not only good for health, but is also healthy for the planet. This chapter discusses the environmental benefits of plant-based eating, along with the various recommendations that have been proposed to achieve a sustainable diet.

Food's Impact on the Environment

Food production is extrinsically linked to the environment. For example a number of agricultural practices impact the environment through land use changes, water availability, energy consumption, fertilizer and pesticide use. However the relationship between food and the environment is intertwined so that environmental changes will in turn effect food production. Figure 9.1 describes this relationship.

However measuring the environmental impact of food production is complex with many factors needing to be considered. Life-cycle analysis (LCA) is a

FIGURE 9.1 – Food's Relationship with the Environment

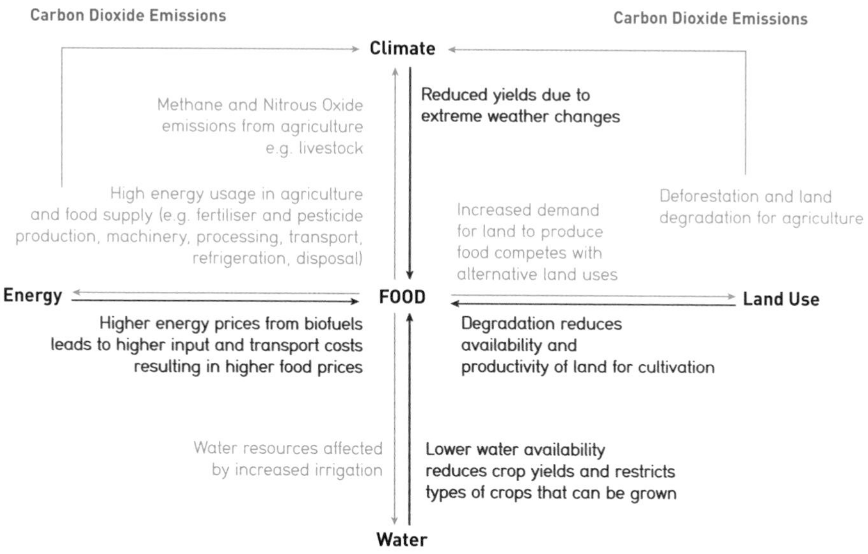

Source: Adapted from Oxfam GB Briefing Paper[4]

method that has been identified to address this. LCA takes into account all stages of food production from farm to fork and includes:

- Agricultural inputs (feed, fertiliser)
- Agriculture itself (food production)
- Food processing/ manufacturing
- Packaging
- Distribution and retail
- Storage
- Consumption
- Land use change arising from agriculture production

The contribution of these different stages to the total environmental impact will depend on the food product, the method used to do the calculations and the impact that is being measured e.g. greenhouse gas emissions (GHGe), water requirements, energy needs, etc. Although LCA is considered the best method for assessing environmental impacts, LCA will take time to complete and are currently not available for all foods.

In the mean time, the following explains how food production and different agricultural practices impact climate change, land use, water and energy resources using currently available data.

Food Production and Climate Change

Global warming is caused primarily by GHGe such as carbon dioxide, methane and nitrous oxide. These gases act like the glass in a greenhouse, trapping heat from the sun to warm up the earth. Although most of these gases occur naturally, and are vital to ensure the planet stays warm enough to sustain life, the balance is very delicate. Current lifestyles are resulting in an increase in GHGe and if this continues the planet's temperature will rise higher and higher. This warming would increase the risk of flooding, droughts, hurricanes, tropical storms as well as a loss in biodiversity. This in turn would damage sectors such as agriculture and ultimately threaten human health. Between 1970 and 2004 global emissions of these three GHG's increased by a colossal 70%[5].

Many experts believe that climate change is the most serious issue facing the human race. As a result various policies such as the United Framework Convention on Climate Change (UNFCCC) and the Kyoto Protocol have been agreed. In terms of Europe:

- 27 countries of the European Union have agreed to a 20% cut in GHGe by 2020 (taking 1990 as the base)
- WWF-UK has also set out targets to reduce GHGe by at least 25% by 2020 (based on 1990 levels) and 70% by 2050 as part of its One Planet Food Programme[6].

Each of the GHG's has a different warming potential with nitrous oxide and methane presenting a much higher risk for the environment (Table 9.1).

TABLE 9.1 – Global Warming Impacts of the GHG

	Carbon Dioxide e.g. from fossil fuels	Methane e.g. from livestock emissions and manure	Nitrous Oxide e.g. from fertiliser
Global Warming Potential	1	21	310

Source: European Parliament Science and Technology Options Assessment[2]

The food system is believed to be a very significant contributor to global GHGe, accounting for approximately 30% of the European Union's total GHGe[7,8]. While calculating GHGe is difficult (due to the complexities of measuring GHGe at the different stages of the LCA), it has been estimated that agriculture, including fertiliser application and production, contributes 12-14% of GHGe.

On a global scale, nitrous oxide from soils and methane from enteric fermentation and manure are the largest sources of GHGe from agriculture. In fact, livestock production globally accounts for 18% of the total GHGe, more than the entire transport system[9]. However this will vary across region to region and also depends on the livestock system used (pastoral versus intensive, as well as the type of livestock).

Various studies have attempted to calculate the GHGe from different food products. For example McMichael calculated in terms of livestock the biggest contributors, are cattle, sheep and pig production (Table 9.2)[10].

TABLE 9.2 – Global Livestock Emissions per Year (Million Tonnes of GHG)

Livestock	Carbon Dioxide	Methane (enteric)	Methane (manure)
Cattle*	1,906	75	8
Sheep and Goats	514	9	0.3
Pigs	590	1	8
Poultry	61	-	1

*Includes dairy cattle which are estimated to be responsible for one quarter of total cattle methane emissions - Source; McMichael, 2007[10]

GHGe from milk, eggs and fish are lower than beef, lamb and pork, but these can increase with processing. In contrast, plant foods have been estimated to produce far fewer GHGe (Table 9.3).

A Swedish study which compared the total GHGe for 22 food items sold in Sweden also found comparable results. In this study plant foods based on vegetables, cereals and legumes generally produced the lowest GHGe (with the exception of those shipped by aeroplane). Also animal products were generally associated with higher GHGe than plant-based products, with the highest emissions occurring in meats from ruminants[11].

TABLE 9.3 – Ranges of GHGe from Various Food Products (kg Carbon Dioxide Equivalents* per kg Product)

Livestock/Crop	Kg Carbon Dioxide eq/kg Product
Cattle (beef)	6.25 – 37.0
Sheep	7.6 - 17
Pigs	3.6 - 6.4
Poultry	1.1- 4.6
Oilseed rape	1.7
Cattle (dairy)	0.41 - 1.38
Soybean meal	0.934
Bread	0.8
Onions/ Cabbages	0.5
Bananas	0.45
Rice	0.4
Wheat	0.32
Oranges	0.25
Apples	0.24
Potato	0.17- 0.24

* Carbon Dioxide equivalents is a measure used to compare the emissions from various greenhouse gases based upon their global warming potential
Source: European Parliament Science and Technology Options Assessment[2]

Another comparison between soya-based foods and animal products found that cow's milk (1.3 kg CO2 Eq/l) created on average five times more carbon dioxide equivalents per litre than soya milk (0.28 kg CO2 Eq/l). While beef generated 10 times more per kilogram than tofu[12]. Studies have also investigated the climatic effect of producing protein from different food sources and concluded that it's more 'climate friendly' to produce protein from vegetable sources than from animal sources (although some animal products are fairly climate efficient). For example the Swedish study described previously found that wheat, local herring and soya beans (cooked and shipped by boat) were the top 3 most climate efficient protein producing foods[11].

As studies use different methods to calculate these GHGe, caution does need to be taken when interpreting this information. However, it's generally agreed that on average meat and dairy products are the most GHG-intensive relative to other food groups, with most emissions coming from the agricultural stage of the LCA[13].

While it's imperative there are technological improvements in the growing, manufacture and distribution of foods to reduce GHGe, this technology will not be sufficient to reach the proposed targets. Changes in what is eaten are also required. A WWF/ Food Climate Research Network report 'How Low Can We Go' (which explores how a 70% reduction in emissions can be achieved), suggested that removing meat from the diet, and replacing it with plant-based foods with a similar protein content, would reduce the Carbon footprint by 20%. Removing all animal products reduces it by about 30%[6].

Another study also considered the potential strategies for the agricultural sector to meet the UK's recommended GHGe targets. In this the authors suggested that as well as technological improvements in agriculture practices, a 30% reduction in livestock production would also be needed. The study further investigated the effect this reduction in consumption would have on health and concluded that it could reduce the burden from Heart Disease by about 15% due to the associated reductions in saturated fat and cholesterol intake[14].

Food Production and Land Use

Land is a valuable commodity and as such it is important to consider the best way to use it. For example it's important to ensure adequate sustenance for the population but consideration must also be given to minimise any environmental damage. Currently 25-30% of the earth's entire land surface (65-70% of all agricultural land) is used for rearing farmed animals. Much of this is used as grazing land however crops are also grown for animal feed. One third of all land that is suitable for growing crops is used to produce feed for farmed animals[9].

Animals such as poultry and pigs consume only grains, whereas cattle and sheep consume both forage and grains. However, livestock animals are relatively inefficient at converting grains to meat, with large amounts of the grain's energy and protein not being used to make animal protein or fat. Consequently large amounts of grain are needed to produce 1kg of meat (Table 9.4). Nevertheless, in certain parts of the world where the land is only suitable for growing grass, it can be argued that there is no alternative but to have ruminants graze on this land to preserve the local eco-system.

TABLE 9.4 – Ranges of Grain Feed Required to Produce 1kg Meat

Pig meat	Poultry	Beef	Mutton
2.64 – 5.9 kg	2 – 4 kg	7 – 13 kg	7 – 21 kg

Source: European Parliament Science and Technology Options Assessment[2]

Rather than growing grains to feed animals it has been suggested that some of these grains would be better used to feed the world's growing population. In fact, in the US, the amount of grains fed to US livestock is sufficient to feed approximately 840 million people who eat a plant-based diet[15].
Soya beans are a major source of protein in animal feed and currently 90% of the world's soya is used in this way. Soya-based feed plays a significant contribution towards land-use change in other parts of the world. However, again this link could be broken if soya was directly consumed by humans. Its excellent nutritional properties and high quality protein (referred to in Chapter 02) make it an ideal food for health and the environment.
One estimate has suggested that a typical meat-based diet requires two and half times more land compared to a vegetarian diet[16].

Food Production and Energy Resources

Although food provides energy, at the same time it requires energy to produce. Key energy inputs for agriculture are fossil fuel for fertilizer production, agricultural machinery, fuel, irrigation and pesticides. Fossil fuel estimates for different food productions have been made by different authors. This data suggests that meat production requires considerably more fossil fuel per kilogram of meat than plant-based food production (Table 9.5).

When energy requirements are considered in relation to the protein and energy content of the food, grains and some legumes e.g. soya beans, are produced more efficiently than vegetables, fruit and animal products. One study calculated that on average to produce 1 kcal of plant protein requires 2.2kcal of fossil energy. In contrast, producing animal protein is more energy intensive requiring 25kcal of fossil fuel to produce 1kcal of meat protein, more than 11 times that of

TABLE 9.5 – Ranges of Fossil Fuel Input Required for Different Food Products (MJ/kg)

Livestock/Crop	Energy input (MJ/kg)
Cattle (beef)	15.5 – 55.56
Pork	17 – 21.06
Sheep	17 – 19.3
Poultry	12 - 25
Eggs	14 – 22.18
Rice	8.82
Soya beans	5.9
Bananas	5.34
Maize	5.13
Pulses	4.88
Wheat	4.03
Cattle (dairy)	2.5 – 3.62
Oranges	2.96
Apples	2.87
Hay	2.77
Oats	2.75
Root crops	2.32
Potatoes	1.17 – 1.4

Source: European Parliament Science and Technology Options Assessment[2]

plant protein[15]. However energy requirements will depend on the type of livestock, the type of feed (grain versus pasture) and the geographic location. The two livestock systems that depend most heavily on forage, but also rely on significant amounts of grain, are beef and lamb. As a result they require the highest amount of energy to produce 1kcal of protein. If these animals were fed on only good quality pasture, the energy inputs could be reduced by about a half[15].

One study has attempted to examine the environmental impact of whole diets rather than individual foods. Data from Seventh Day Adventists in California was used to compare vegetarian and non-vegetarian diets. Among the 34,000 Californian Adventists participating in the Adventist Health Study I cohort around 50% were vegetarians and 50% were non-vegetarians. Dietary information, collected from the study questionnaire, found that non-vegetarians ate substantially more animal foods than the vegetarians, whereas the vegetarians ate slightly more plant foods. Using environmental information from state agricultural data it was found that the non-vegetarian diet required 2.5 times more energy, 13 times more fertilizer and 1.4 times more pesticides than the vegetarian diet[17].

Food Production and Water

More fresh water is used for agriculture than any other human activity. It has been suggested that if current trends for water continue 47% of the world's population will live in areas of water stress by 2030[2].

The water required to produce various food and feed crops ranges from 500 to 3000 litres of water per kilogram of crop produced. If irrigation systems are needed, this amount can increase considerably. Producing 1kg of animal protein requires about 100 times more water than producing 1kg of grain protein. The actual amount of water that is drunk directly by livestock is very small (1.3% of the total water used in agriculture). However, when the water to make the feed and forage is taken into account this volume increases dramatically[15]. Different animals vary in the amount of water required for their production. Other factors that will determine how much water is required include geographic location (how much rainfall there is), as well their type of feed and where this is grown. A number of estimates have been calculated to determine the amount of water required for different foods. These ranges of are summarised in Table 9.6.

In terms of the water impact in relation to whole diets, data from the previously described Adventist Health Study concluded that the non-vegetarian diet requires 2.9 times more water than the vegetarian diet[17].

A further issue of agricultural practices is the potential risk of water pollution. Animal waste, pesticides and fertilisers, at high concentrations, can act as pollutants and should they enter waterways can have a damaging effect on aquatic life and may be partly responsible for 'dead zones' in oceans and rivers where plant and animal life can not exist.

TABLE 9.6 – Agricultural Water Requirement (Litre / kg)

Livestock / Crop	Litre / kg
Beef cattle	12,560 – 43,000
Sheep	4,500 – 6,100
Pig	4,460 – 5,906
Eggs	2,700 – 4,657
Poultry	2,390 – 4,500
Soya bean	1,800 – 3,200
Rice	1,400 – 3,600
Wheat	900 - 2000
Dairy cattle	560 - 1000
Maize	450 - 900
Vegetables	190 – 1,160
Apples	500 - 700
Oranges	500
Potato	105 - 500

Source: European Parliament Science and Technology Options Assessment[2]

What is a Sustainable Diet?

A definition of sustainability has been suggested as 'capable of being maintained over the long term and meeting the needs of the present, without compromising the ability of future generations to meet their needs'[18]. However defining a sustainable diet is complex and as yet no universal definition has been agreed. Consideration needs to be given to the health benefits, environmental sustainability, economic stability as well as social aspects. While it is beyond the scope of this chapter to discuss every element that must be considered, environmental sustainability mainly focuses on resource depletion, land use change, biodiversity and GHGe as described in this chapter.

Bringing health and environmental sustainability together is now becoming an important priority for both the scientific community and policy makers. Some countries such as Germany and Sweden have drawn up official guidelines. In the UK, the UK Sustainable Development Commission (UK SDC) has drawn up recommendations which consider both public health nutrition as well as environmental sustainability. One of the highest priority changes in this guidance was to reduce the consumption of meat and dairy foods[19]. Recommendations by other organisations reinforce this advice (Table 9.7).

TABLE 9.7 – Recommendations by Various Organisations to Reduce Meat and Dairy Consumption

Organisation	Report	Recommendations
UK SDC[19]	Setting The Table; Advice to Government on priority elements of sustainable diets	Reduce meat and dairy consumption
Oxfam[4]	Oxfam GB Briefing Paper – 4-a-week. Changing food consumption in the UK to benefit people and planet	Reduce consumption of meat and dairy products
Food Climate Research Network[13]	Cooking up a storm: Food, greenhouse gas emissions and our changing climate.	'Eating fewer meat and dairy products and consuming more plant foods in their place is probably the single most helpful behaviour shift one can make.'
WWF-UK[20]	Livewell plate	Eat more fruit, vegetables and cereals (especially regionally grown, in season) Eat less meat (meat of all kinds – red and white – are a "hotspot" in terms of environmental impact)
American Dietetic Association (ADA)[18]	Position of the ADA: Food and Nutrition Professionals Can Implement Practices to Conserve Natural Resources and Support Ecological Sustainability	Encourage consumption of protein from plant sources

How can this be put into practice? Although many experts agree on the need to cut down on meat and dairy consumption, they do not need to be eliminated completely from the diet. Nevertheless current consumption of many of these foods is higher than the dietary recommendations for good health (see Chapter 01). In fact, if consumption was in line with these recommendations a significant step towards a low carbon diet would be achieved. This was highlighted in the recent WWF-UK report "Livewell - a balance of healthy and sustainable food choices'[20].

They concluded that '*a diet can be achieved which meets dietary recommendations for health and the GHGE reduction targets for 2020, without eliminating all meat and dairy products. Rebalancing the UK diet in line with the Eatwell plate and reducing meat-based proteins could achieve a diet that would meet the 2020 GHGe target.*'

This is the first attempt at defining a sustainable diet, and whilst it's recognised that it's not perfect, it's the first step towards a sustainable diet which can be built upon. In the future it can take into account wider environmental impacts as well as social and ethical aspects.

Another quantifiable target has been proposed by McMichael et al. who have suggested a global target of 90g of meat/ person/ day, of this, no more than 50g should come from red meat products[10]. Although it's difficult to compare this target with current intake (see Chapter 01), based on the available European data, most countries would need to reduce their intakes to reach this target.

Conclusions

If the planet is to be protected, a number of changes are needed including technological improvements in the growth, manufacture, distribution, storage and preparation of food. However if targets, such as GHGe, are to be met this will not be enough. For this reason a number of experts are also recommending different eating patterns. Eating more plant-based foods, and reducing meat and dairy foods, are small changes that will have a big impact on our planet.

Eating plant-based foods rather than animal-based foods can contribute to a healthier planet.

Animal-derived foods generally require more resources than plant-based foods.

Shifting towards plant-based eating, while cutting down on animal foods, can make a big difference to both our health and the planet's.

Literature chapter 09

1. FAO, United Nations Population Division.
2. European Parliament Science and Technology Options Assessment, Implications of global trends in eating habits for climate change, health and natural resources. 2008. **IP/A/STOA/2008-04**.
3. Worldwatch Institute, State of the World 2008: Innovations for a Sustainable Economy.
4. Oxfam GB Briefing Paper. 4-a-week. Changing food consumption in the UK to benefit people and planet. 2009 March 2011]; Available from: http://www.oxfam.org.uk/resources/policy/climate_change/downloads/ogb_bp_4aweek.pdf.
5. Intergovernmental Panel on Climate Change. 2007 March 2011]; Available from: www.ipcc.ch.
6. Audsley, E., Brander, M., Chatterton, J., Murphy-Bokern, D., Webster, C., and Williams, A., How Low Can We Go? An assessment of greenhouse gas emissions from the UK food system and the scope to reduce them by 2050. 2009, FCRN-WWF-UK.
7. European Commission, Environmental impact of products (EIPRO): Analysis of the life cycle environmental impacts related to the total final consumption of the EU 25., in European Commission Technical Report EUR 22284 EN. 2006, European Commission: Brussels.
8. Foresight, The Future of Food and Farming. 2011, Government Office For Science, London.
9. Food and Agriculture Organisation of the United Nations, Livestock's Long Shadow - Environmental Issues and Options. . 2006: Rome.
10. McMichael, A.J., et al., Food, livestock production, energy, climate change, and health. Lancet, 2007. 370(9594): p. 1253-63.
11. Carlsson-Kanyama, A. and A.D. Gonzalez, Potential contributions of food consumption patterns to climate change. Am J Clin Nutr, 2009. 89(5): p. 1704S-1709S.
12. Alpro calculations (Ecofys) 2009.
13. Garnett, T., Cooking up a storm: Food, greenhouse gas emissions and our changing climate. 2008, Food Climate Research Network, Centre for Environmental Strategy, University of Surrey.
14. Friel, S., et al., Public health benefits of strategies to reduce greenhouse-gas emissions: food and agriculture. Lancet, 2009. 374(9706): p. 2016-25.
15. Pimentel, D. and M. Pimentel, Sustainability of meat-based and plant-based diets and the environment. Am J Clin Nutr, 2003. 78(3 Suppl): p. 660S-663S.
16. Zollitsch W, e.a., Sustainable food production and ethics. 2007: Wageningen Academic Publishers.
17. Marlow, H.J., et al., Diet and the environment: does what you eat matter? Am J Clin Nutr, 2009. 89(5): p. 1699S-1703S.
18. Harmon, A.H. and B.L. Gerald, Position of the American Dietetic Association: food and nutrition professionals can implement practices to conserve natural resources and support ecological sustainability. J Am Diet Assoc, 2007. 107(6): p. 1033-43.
19. Sustainable Development Commission, Setting The Table; Advice to Government on priority elements of sustainable diets. 2009.
20. WWF, Livewell: a balance of healthy and sustainable food choices. January 2011.

10

Chapter 10

Plant-Based Eating in Practice

Summary

- Plant-based eating is considered a solution to the growing health and environmental challenges now being faced.
- Although there is universal consensus that more plant foods should be eaten in the diet, this can be perceived as difficult to achieve.
- Reasons given for not adopting a plant-based eating plan include a lack of awareness of what this way of eating involves, concerns about radically changing existing eating habits, as well as the lack of plant-based eating options when eating out.
- Nutrition professionals are in an ideal position to educate people on plant-based eating and support them in making permanent changes to their dietary habits.
- There's more than one way to include more plant foods into the diet including reshaping what's on the plate, making simple dietary swaps, giving meals a plant make-over and opting for meat free days.
- Making changes to include more plant foods should be undertaken gradually by setting small, realistic goals on a regular basis.
- Setting small goals and building upon these over time is more likely to result in a permanent shift to plant-based eating.

Throughout this book the health and the environmental benefits of plant-based eating have been clearly identified. This way of eating is not another fad diet; instead it is a real solution to the growing health and environmental challenges we are now facing. Plant-based eating is not about transforming the diet but about making small changes to put plant-based foods first.
Despite the quite clear advantages of eating more plant-based foods, studies have found that people perceive this to be difficult to achieve in practice. In one Australian study the main barriers identified included:

- Lack of information – both on the definition of plant-based eating and on the potential benefits of this way of eating, especially in relation to the environment;
- Not wanting to alter eating habits – as well as eating habits of individuals, there were also concerns that family members wouldn't want to eat a plant-based regime;
- Lack of availability of plant-based options when eating out.

It's important to address these barriers if plant foods are to be increased in the diet. Yet in this study there was higher agreement with the benefits of plant-based eating than there was with the potential barriers of such a diet. Furthermore, 62% of respondents were interested in learning more about plant-based eating[1].

Nutrition professionals are in an ideal position to help people adopt a plant-based eating pattern. They have the skills to translate the science into meaningful information people understand; they are able to discuss potential barriers and provide solutions to overcome these difficulties; and they can provide practical suggestions including shopping, preparing and cooking ideas. All in all they can help people change their eating habits for good, enabling plant-based eating to become a permanent feature of the diet.
This chapter provides practical suggestions and solutions to help health professionals promote plant-based eating. It's not intended to be a rigid diet. Instead the aim of a plant-based eating plan is to be flexible so that people can include more plant foods based on their likes and dislikes and taking into account their lifestyles.

Getting Started...

When considering a change in any eating habit it's important for an individual to identify the benefits they would gain by making dietary changes. In the same way, people need to think about the personal advantages they could obtain by moving towards plant-based eating. Everyone will have different reasons. For one it may be to lose weight. For another it may be to feel healthier. While for some it may be the contribution they are making to the environment.
Table 10.1 lists some of the benefits that have been highlighted in the previously described Australian study that investigated consumers' readiness to eat a plant-based diet. Here, reasons were grouped into four main sections – well-being benefits; weight and health benefits; ethical benefits; and convenience and financial benefits.

TABLE 10.1 – Perceived Benefits of Eating a Plant-based Diet

Well-being benefits	• Have a better quality of life • Stay healthy • Be fit • Have a tasty diet • Have plenty of energy • Eat a more 'natural' diet • Improve digestion • Eat a greater variety of foods • Have lots of vitamins and minerals
Weight and health benefits	• Decrease saturated fat intake • Control weight • Prevent disease in general • Eat more fibre
Ethical benefits	• Help the environment • Decrease hunger in the Third World • Help animal welfare/rights • Increase efficiency of food production
Convenience and Financial benefits	• Save time • Have fewer food storage problems • Save money • Eat a greater variety of foods • Have a tasty diet

Source: Lea EJ, et al[2]

It may be useful for people to write down the benefits that are appropriate to them and use these as a constant reminder to keep motivated.
At the same time, it's also essential to help individuals identify any potential difficulties they foresee in including more plant foods into their diet. Strategies

for overcoming these will need to be discussed, as the benefits of change need to outweigh the perceived barriers if plant-based eating is to become a permanent feature in the diet. Table 10.2 describes some of the potential barriers to plant-based eating highlighted in the Australian study.

TABLE 10.2 – Potential Barriers to Plant-based Eating

Personal barriers	• Lack of information on plant-based eating • Not wanting to change eating habits or routine • Wouldn't get enough energy • Not tasty enough • Not enough choice when eating out • Inconvenient
Family and convenience barriers	• Family members not wanting to eat a plant-based diet • Takes too long to prepare • Not knowing how to prepare plant-based meals
Health barriers	• Not enough iron in them • Not enough protein in them • Concern about getting indigestion, bloating, gas or flatulence • Concern about the need to eat large amounts of plant foods
'Junk' food, shopping, eating out and financial barriers	• Concern about having to go shopping more often • Would miss eating lots of junk food • Too expensive • Not enough choice when eating out
Information barriers	• The need for more information about plant-based diets • Not knowing how to prepare plant-based meals • Not knowing what to eat instead of lots of meat • Not filling enough • Need to eat large quantities

Source: Lea EJ, et al[2]

Interestingly, the barriers that were cited in the first study by Lea were not the same as those that have been given for adopting a vegetarian diet. It was suggested that this maybe because animal foods are still included in plant-based eating and it maybe that consumers perceive switching to a plant-based diet as a smaller step than switching to a vegetarian diet[1].

Once these pros and cons have been weighed up and its been concluded that eating more plant-based foods is the way forward, then the next step is to identify how this can be achieved. A good starting point is to determine the foods that are currently being consumed so that possible areas for change can be identified. A food diary is a useful tool to do this. Ideally all food and drink that have been consumed for a week should be recorded, along with the times when eaten. The amounts of animal products, fruits, vegetables and whole-grain cereals consumed each week can be determined from these diaries and intakes compared to the recommended amounts for these foods (see Chapter 01).

Explaining a Plant-based Eating Plan

One of the main barriers to adopting a plant-based eating plan is not being aware of what this way of eating entails. It is important to stress that this is not about giving up animal foods, but it involves putting plant foods first. Table 10.3 describes the main plant foods that should form the bulk of a plant-based way of eating.

TABLE 10.3 – Plant-based Foods

Food Groups	Food Examples
Whole-grains	Wholemeal bread, whole-grain breakfast cereal, oats, brown rice, wholemeal pasta, popcorn, whole-grain rice cakes, rye crisp breads, oatcakes
Legumes including soya	Beans such as kidney beans, black eyed beans, baked beans, soya beans, edamame beans Peas, chickpeas and lentils
Soya products	Fortified soya milk, soya yoghurts and desserts, tofu, meat variations (soya burgers, soya mince)
Vegetables	Fresh vegetables, salad vegetables, tinned vegetables, frozen vegetables
Fruits	Fresh fruit, fruit juice, dried fruit, fruit smoothies, tinned fruit in natural juices, frozen fruit
Nuts and Seeds	Almonds, peanuts, walnuts, cashews, sunflower seeds, pumpkin seeds, linseeds, flaxseeds, peanut butter, tahini

Putting It into Practice

Once eating habits have been identified and plant-based eating has been described, the next stage is to consider what dietary changes need to be made. The first step is to ensure that an individual is eating the right balance of foods.

Eating according to national food based dietary guidelines (see Chapter 01) would be the first phase towards eating more plant foods. Once this has been established, more plant foods can gradually be incorporated into the diet. However not knowing how to practically incorporate these foods into the diet is another barrier given to plant-based eating. It should be stressed that a plant-based eating plan is not a 'one-diet-fits-all'. Instead personalised, practical advice needs to be tailored around the individual. As such there is more than one way to adopting a plant-based eating plan and depending on the individual they may decide to try one or more of these suggestions. For example:

1. Reshaping the plate

Consider what makes up a meal. Often meat tends to be the main focus of meals, yet by addressing the balance on a plate, more room can be made for plant foods. The World Cancer Research Fund (WCRF) has suggested that at least two-thirds of a plate should be made up of plant foods (vegetables, whole-grains, cereals and pulses) and foods from animals should make up less than a third[3]. This can be achieved by suggesting people visualise their plate divided into thirds (Figure 10.1). If meat is the major focus, recommendations can be made to shift towards smaller servings with larger portions of vegetables and whole-grains, or replacements for meat can be selected from the ideas given in Table 10.4.

FIGURE 10.1 – A plant-based plate

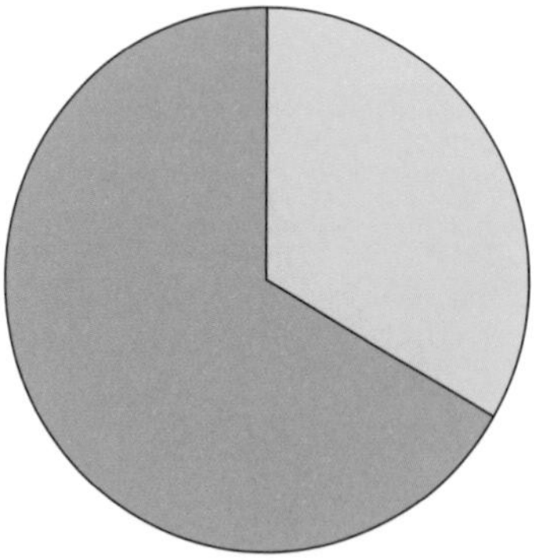

Alternatively when people are planning their meals suggest they consider the plant foods such as whole-grains, vegetables and pulses first of all, and then think how meat can be served as an accompaniment around these foods.

2. Simple Swaps

There are now plenty of plant-based foods available which can be eaten instead of animal foods. Table 10.4 provides some suggestions.

TABLE 10.4 – Simple Swaps to Promote Plant-based Eating

Instead of...	Swap to...
Dairy products e.g. milk, yoghurts, milkshakes, etc	Soya dairy alternatives e.g. soya drink, soya yoghurts, soya shakes
Snacks such as crisps, sweets, chocolates and biscuits	Snacks such as fresh or dried fruit; fruit smoothie; soya shakes; soya nuts; other unsalted nuts; seeds; whole-grain cereal bars; rice cakes; pitta/vegetable sticks/oatcakes with hummus or salsa; plain popcorn.
White bread, pasta and rice	Wholemeal bread, whole-grain pasta and brown rice
Refined breakfast cereals	Whole-grain cereals
Butter	Margarines made from vegetable oils
Lard	Vegetable oils such as olive oil, rapeseed oil, sunflower oil
Creamy meat based pasta sauce	Tomato and vegetable based pasta sauce
Mince, burgers, sausages, etc	Meat variations such as soya mince, Quorn, veggie burgers and sausages
Meat/chicken-based curries or Chinese dishes	Vegetable curries, dhal, mushroom/edamame stir fries and noodle dishes
Desserts/Puddings	Soya yoghurts, soya desserts, fruit crumble (topping made with wholemeal flour and oats) served with soya custard, stewed fruit topped with soya cream alternative

3. Meal makeovers

Many familiar meals can easily be based around plant foods. Most people have between five and ten dishes they cook regularly and these can be used to include more plant foods. In this way the whole family can enjoy plant-based eating. For example:

- Meat can be reduced and replaced with vegetables and pulses in chilli-con-carne, stir fries, spaghetti Bolognese, shepherds pie, curries, stews, pasta sauces, etc. Cooking in this way will result in the same quantity of foods being consumed but in a healthier balance.
- Instead of using all meat mince in meals, why not try replacing half of this with soya mince?
- When buying a joint of meat don't just use it for one meal but think how it can be used for several. For example by serving smaller amounts of roast beef with lots of vegetables, there will be leftovers to make a beef curry and/ or Bolognese sauce and/ or beef chilli. Alternatively left over roast chicken can be used for chicken sandwiches and/or Mexican chicken tortilla wraps and/or chicken soup and/or sweet and sour chicken. The chicken carcase can then be made into homemade chicken stock. Alternatively if the thought of having the same meat on a number of consecutive days is unappealing, any leftovers can be frozen. These can then make a quick nutritious meal for days when time is short.
- Seeds and/or nuts can be added to salads instead of cheese or bacon bits.

These are just a few suggestions. For further on-line support which is full of practical suggestions, as well as useful tips, to make a nutritious yet delicious Plant-based Eating Plan visit
www.plantaardigplan.be,
www.derpflanzlicheplan.de,
www.plantbasedeating.co.uk,
www.visionvegetale.be,
www.plantaardigplan.nl,
www.plantbasedeating.eu.

Although it's not necessary to become vegetarian when following a plant-based eating plan, it might be worthwhile considering buying a vegetarian cook book. This can give further ideas on how to include more grains, vegetables and pulses at meals.

4. Meat-free days

Some people are now deciding to keep one or more days of the week meat free. While this is another strategy for cutting down on animal foods, people should be advised on suitable plant alternatives during these times to ensure the meals are nutritionally adequate.

5. Eating out

In today's busy lifestyle a number of meals are now eaten when out and about. As this is also cited as a barrier to eating more plant-based foods, suggestions should be provided on suitable options. Here are just a few suggestions, although many more will be available depending on the eating establishment.

LIGHT BITES

- Jacket potatoes topped with
  - baked beans
  - or spicy Mexican beans
  - or tuna and sweetcorn
- Sandwiches with
  - a falafel and salad filling
  - or avocado, salad and pine-nut filling
- Vegetable/mushroom/ bean soups with a crusty wholemeal roll
- Salads such as
  - Tomato based pasta salad
  - Couscous salad with roasted vegetables
  - Three bean salad
- Vegetarian burger on a wholemeal roll with lettuce and tomato

MAIN DINNERS

Try to choose somewhere where there are lots of plant-based options on the menu, for example

- Spanish paella
- Asian stir fries
- Italian pasta sauces such as Napoletena, primavera, provencale, puttanesca
- Spicy Indian dhals
- Vegetable pizza

Whatever way a person chooses to include more plant foods into the diet, planning will be crucial if people are to maintain dietary changes. People may therefore need further advice on shopping smartly, recipe and meal planning, cooking tips as well as guidance on the nutritional adequacy of the diet.

Setting Goals

Once consideration has been given to the dietary changes needed to include more plant foods into the diet, the next stage is to set some goals based on these changes. Setting goals plays an important role when changing eating habits. Reaching goals helps to boost confidence, keeps motivation high and increases the chance of success. Goals need to be achievable and realistic. Setting a few to begin with works best. These can gradually be built upon over time. It's important to stress that it's not about making radical changes to the diet; instead, by gradually building up the intake of plant foods it's more likely that this eating pattern will end up becoming permanent.

When setting goals they should be considered in the context of being SMART –

Specific – need to be targeted, not vague, and stating what will be eaten

Measurable – needs to have a time period i.e. how many days this will be done for

Achievable – they should be challenging but they also have to be achievable

Realistic – they need to be relevant to the individual

Timely – a time period should be set when the goal can be reviewed

It's useful for people to write down their goals, along with the steps they need to take to reach this goal e.g.

GOAL: To eat a total of five portions of fruit and vegetables every day

STEPS TO ACHIEVE THIS OVER THE NEXT 4 WEEKS:

1. Buy more fruit and vegetables when shopping
2. Have a glass of fruit juice at breakfast
3. Take fruit to work to have as snacks
4. To have salad in the lunchtime sandwich
5. Have at least 2 different types of vegetables in the evening meal

These goals should be reflected on regularly. Making slow, gradual changes will mean these changes are more likely to become a permanent part of the everyday diet. It will also help the body get accustomed to the dietary changes, as plant-based eating will probably contain more fibre than people are used too. This is important to highlight, as while eating more fibre is beneficial in its own right, it can result in bloating, flatulence, etc in the short term until the body adjusts to the changes in the diet.

Keep Going

After reaching the first set of goals, hopefully people will be feeling the benefit. At this stage, it can be tempting for them to revert back to their old eating habits, however they should be encouraged not to stop. Once the first set of goals have been reached, they should keep to these and set themselves new goals. If they haven't reached all their goals, they shouldn't panic. They've started the journey and they should be reminded that habits take time to change. They need to be praised for the good work that has been achieved so far and reminded that each extra serving of plant foods is a step in the right direction. There maybe days when they don't 'get it right', but they shouldn't be too hard on themselves. Lapses are an inevitable part of change; however it's important not to let one slip into another. Reflect on why things haven't been going according to the plan and make the necessary changes to get back on track.

Gradually old habits will become a thing of the past and changes to include more plant foods will form new habits. In this way people will settle into the same comfortable relationships with this way of eating as they had with their older, unhealthier habits.

Eating more plant foods is both environmentally and health friendly.

It's important to consider the benefits of plant-based eating, as well as how to overcome any potential barriers, if dietary changes are to become permanent habits.

Use a food diary to identify areas of the diet that can be changed to include more plant foods.

Set SMART goals which can be gradually built upon over time.

Making slow, gradual changes to include plant foods is more likely to result in these changes being a permanent feature of the diet.

For further advice on how to practically include more plant-based foods into the diet please visit www.plantaardigplan.be, www.derpflanzlicheplan.de, www.plantbasedeating.co.uk, www.visionvegetale.be, www.plantaardigplan.nl, www.plantbasedeating.eu.

Literature chapter 10

1. Lea, E.J., D. Crawford, and A. Worsley, Public views of the benefits and barriers to the consumption of a plant-based diet. Eur J Clin Nutr, 2006. 60(7): p. 828-37.
2. Lea, E.J., D. Crawford, and A. Worsley, Consumers' readiness to eat a plant-based diet. Eur J Clin Nutr, 2006. 60(3): p. 342-51.
3. World Cancer Research Fund/American Institute for Cancer Research, Food, Nutrition, and Physical Activity, and the Prevention of Cancer: A Global Perspective., in Washington, DC: AICR. 2007.

Conclusion

- For centuries many people's traditional diets have been based on plant foods and it is this particular feature which is thought to contribute to their markedly good health and long life.
- As societies have become more affluent there has been a shift from these traditional diets to a more 'Western' style of eating and instead of plant foods, animal foods have become the central focus of meals and menus in this way of eating.
- Associated with this eating pattern is a diet typically high in fat, especially saturated fat, and low in fibre. This nutritional intake is linked with lifestyle diseases such as heart disease, diabetes and obesity which are now major challenges in many European countries.
- Many international dietary recommendations emphasise plant foods to promote good health as experts believe that increasing the amount of plant foods, and eating smaller amounts of animal foods, would be beneficial for health.
- Currently there is no precise definition of a plant-based diet but this way of eating does not necessarily exclude all animal products, instead it places the emphasis on plant foods.
- The 5 major plant-based food groups that should be the focus of plant-based eating include, whole-grains, legumes – including soya, fruit, vegetables, nuts and seeds.
- Plant-based eating patterns tend to be low in total fat and saturated fat, include a good level of unsaturated fats leading to better overall fat quality, and are high in fibre – all in line with the international and national dietary recommendations.
- Many plant-based foods also contain polyphenols and are typically rich sources of a variety of vitamins and minerals, important for good health.
- Specific plant foods or ingredients such as soya protein, nuts, oat/ barley beta glucan may further provide additional health benefits.
- The nutritional characteristics of plant-based eating are thought to be responsible for the healthier hearts, body weights and blood sugar levels observed in people whose diets are mainly based on plant foods.
- As a result there is convincing evidence that plant-based eaters have a lower prevalence of obesity, lower rates of coronary heart disease and probably lower rates of hypertension and diabetes.

- Plant-based eating is also considered part of the solution to the growing environmental challenges now being faced. There is evidence that plant foods are more sustainable than animal foods requiring less land, water and energy resources and produce fewer greenhouse gas emissions.
- A sustainable diet that is good for the planet, as well as health, requires a change in eating practices including consuming more plant-based foods and eating fewer meat and dairy products.
- Nutrition professionals are in an ideal position to educate people on plant-based eating and support them in making permanent changes to their dietary habits.
- The wide variety of plant foods available provides a number of options for designing a healthy plant-based eating plan to suit all tastes and palettes for all ages.
- Making changes to include more plant foods should be undertaken gradually by setting small, realistic goals on a regular basis. In this way it's more likely that these changes will become a permanent feature of the diet.
- There's more than one way to include more plant foods into the diet including reshaping what's on the plate, making simple dietary swaps, giving meals a plant make-over and opting for meat free days.
- Appropriately planned plant-based eating patterns which include fruits, vegetables, legumes, whole grains, nuts and seeds are both healthy and can meet the nutritional requirements throughout the lifecycle.

For further advice on how to practically include more plant-based foods into the diet please visit:

BE — Het Plantaardig Plan – www.plantaardigplan.be
DU — Der pflanzliche Plan – www.derpflanzlicheplan.de
UK — Plant-based Eating – www.plantbasedeating.co.uk
FR — Vision Végétale – www.visionvegetale.be
NL — Het Plantaardig Plan – www.plantaardigplan.nl
EU — Plant-based Eating – www.plantbasedeating.eu